मपरेस्त्विनान् रथमारोपयांचक्रे कन्यास्ता भरतर्षभ वीर्यशुल्काश्च

थंतदा श्रवेवंपार्थि
गनान् भीष्मः शांतन
नःपुनः तेपतद्धंपरं
पार्थिवाः प्रसह्याहि
नरर्षभाः ततस्तेष्ट
रुदायुधाः योगोयोग
भ्यचोदयन् तेरथैर्म
जयोधिनः पुष्टैश्चा
सेतुरुदायुधाः तत
वेणवविशांपते रथ
पर्यवारयन् तानहं

The Indian Art Of War

The Mahabharata Paradigm

SHARADA publishing house
delhi

The Indian Art Of War

The Mahabharata Paradigm

(Quest for an Indian Strategic Culture)

Brigadier G.D. Bakshi
VSM

विहदयं वैमनष्यं वदामित्रेषु दुन्दुभे
विद्वेषं कश्मशं भयममित्रेषु नि
दध्मस्यवैनान् दुन्दुभे जहि।

अथर्व वेद

"Speak to our enemies, O wardrum
Faint heartedness and discord of minds
We bring upon our adversaries
Hatred, Panic and division"

Atharva Veda

First Published 2002

ISBN : 81-85618-81-7

Published by
B.L. Bansal
for SHARADA PUBLISHING HOUSE
(Publishers on India's Past & Present)
40, Anand Nagar, Inderlok
Delhi-110035
Ph. : 3657538

Typeset at Balaji Computers, # 7108270

Printed at Santosh Offset, Delhi-35

Dedicated to
Swami Pranvananda Saraswati
to my Parents
and
to George Tanham
In the hope that he will now
See the outlines of a historic
Indian Strategic Culture

Contents

ले जनरल विजय ओबराय
पी वी एस एम, ए वी एस एम, वी एस एम
Lt General Vijay Oberoi
PVSM, AVSM, VSM

सेना मुख्यालय
नई दिल्ली - 110 011
ARMY HEADQUARTERS
NEW DELHI - 110 011

Foreword

The Mahabharata has fascinated the Indian mind for centuries, nay millennia. It has been referred to variously as a cultural heritage, a brilliant story which has all the ingredients of literary genius, a history, a myth and so on, but the military context of Mahabharata has hardly been explored. Brigadier GD Bakshi, VSM, seems to have done just that – an exploration and an analysis of Mahabharata from the military point of view. This is his second book on the subject, the first being 'Mahabharata – A Military Analysis'. In the present book, he has attempted to take his analysis to a higher plane and hence the focus on 'The Indian Art of War'.

The controversy on the classification of Mahabharata, as a myth or otherwise, will no doubt continue, but the author has attempted to project the epic as the 'primary' source book of Indian military thought and tradition. The antiquity of Mahabharata, no doubt qualifies it as the 'primary source book', whether it portrays 'Indian military thought' is for the reader to judge, helped no doubt by the logic and arguments proferred by the author, in this lucid and easily-understood book.

The author has theorized that the fascination of the Indian military with 'attrition', which sadly continues to prevail even today, can be traced to the Mahabharata, which nearly three millenniums ago, outlined an 'attrition-oriented Indian paradigm of war', that was primarily centred on a pure 'force on force' regime. The armies of that period had evolved from the two basic arms of the Early Vedic Period (Infantry and Chariots), to a highly sophisticated four arms structure, comprising Chariots, Elephants, Cavalry and Infantry. Surprisingly, this military organizational format was to remain constant in India till almost the Tenth Century AD. The Chariots were the prize arm of the Mahabharata era. The Mahabharata mentions 'vyuhas', or battle arrays, and battle drills that coordinated the actions of these four variable speed manoeuvre masses, on the battlefield. The prime aim was the destruction and annihilation of the enemy, through systematic attrition.

In the 3rd century BC, a major clash of civilizations occurred between the Greek and Indic Civilizations. Alexander's invasion confronted the Indians with a 'mobility-based' paradigm of war, that came as a great shock to the Indian Armies, which were primed for 'set piece battles' of attrition, in pre-designated battle lines. During the Mauryan era, Kautilya (the redoubtable Chanakya) reflected deeply on these early encounters with the Greeks. He found that the prized Indian Arm of the Chariots was unsuited for mobile operations and cross-country movements. He therefore phased out this Arm and placed heavy reliance on the mass employment of war elephants, to generate 'shock action'. Consequently, the strength of the Elephant Corps of the Mauryan Army was raised from 3000 to 9000 war beasts. What is far more important, however, is the fact that Kautilya waged a brilliant Information Warfare Campaign, to exploit the shock effect of this new weapon system viz the elephants. He wove brilliant psychological themes that exploited the Greek terror of these war beasts. The upshot was that the Greek Army mutinied and refused to go any further. *Kautilya, therefore, appears to emerge as the world's first and most consummate grand master of information warfare.*

Subsequently, Kautilya transformed the 'attrition-oriented' Kshatriya paradigm of the Mahabharata (where attrition was supreme) to the Brahmanical concept of war, based on information dominance and extended covert action campaigns, designed to destabilize and unbalance an enemy, before launching a conventional attack. However, the concept of information dominance started languishing thereafter, and attrition warfare regained its primacy. In recent times, the British reinforced it and therefore it continues to remain the dominant Indian cultural mindset for war fighting, even today. Brief interludes of brilliance (like Kautilya's), were followed by regression to this attrition-based paradigm of the Mahabharata. It is with us to this day, as a basic historical inheritance, although efforts are now afoot to allocate to 'manoeuvre' the predominance it deserves.

In this book, Brig GD Bakshi has attempted to take an objective look at the military and strategic content of the Mahabharata. He has also attempted to relate it to the development of military art in Sun Tzu's China – a civilization of matching scale and antiquity.

Some years ago, American scholars like George Tanham and Stephen P Rosen had researched Indian history in their quest for a historic Indian strategic culture or an Indian way of war. They concluded, sadly, that there was none. Brigadier Bakshi's book attempts to negate their conclusions. It insists that there **is** indeed an Indian paradigm of war, and the Mahabharata Epic provides us a clear insight into this historical Indian way of war. An understanding of this historical inheritance will perhaps assist military thinkers in modern India to evolve military theories and doctrine that suit the innate cultural genius of India.

The book, 'The Indian Art of War' would have achieved its purpose if it spurts further analysis and research by Indologists, in this fascinating field. I commend Brigadier Bakshi for his dedication and diligence in addressing a path-breaking subject and producing a document, which will interest not only a defence analyst but also a historian and indeed even a lay reader, whose intention is only to imbibe knowledge.

New Delhi
22 Mar., 2001

(Vijay Oberoi)
VCOAS, Lt. Gen

An Interesting Comparison

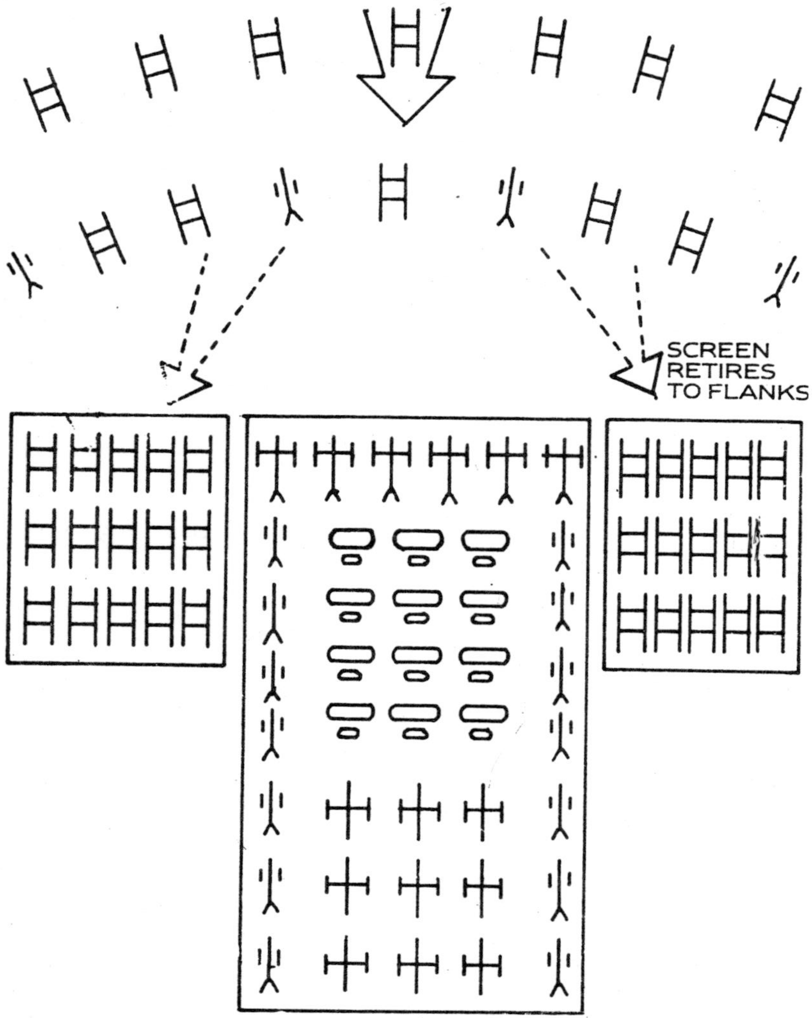

'T' Shaped Lagger Formation Adopted
by Field Marshal Rommels Panzers in World War II

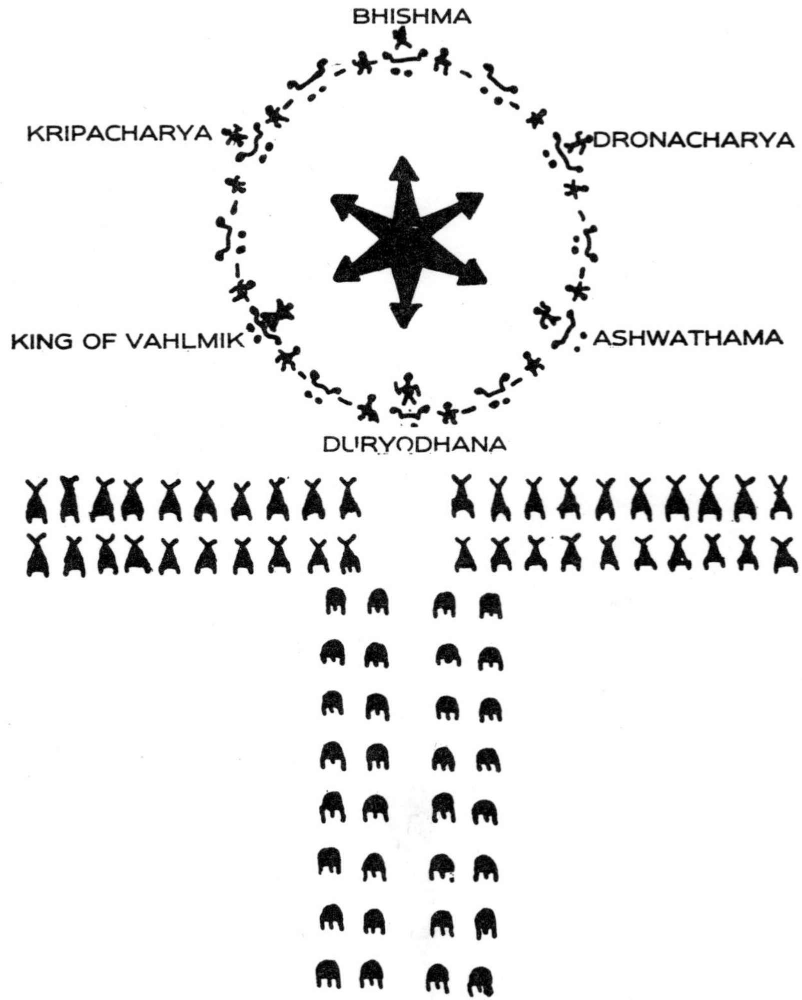

'T' Shaped Sarbatomukha Vyuha
Employed in Mahabharata War

Introductory Note

Dr. G.N. Pant

On 14 September 1975, Dr DC Sircar, one of the most eminent epigraphists of India, declared unequivocally that the *Mahabharata* was a myth, devoid of historicity, opening as it were, the floodgates of controversy all over the country. Professor HD Sankalia, the renowned archaeologists, added fuel to the fire saying that it was only a family feud and belonged to a time when the result of a battle depended primarily on individual strength and prowess as was also the case in ancient Greece and Troy. To him the literary references of the *Mahabharata* are incidental and they are not to be taken at their face value.

The *Mahabharata* categorizes itself as *itihasa* (history) and not as *gatha, akhyana* or *purana*. It comprises a core legend of the family feud leading to the Kurukshetra War, around which were interwoven, in stages, several legends, all mythicized in course of time. The epic *Mahabharata* is a precious document of Indian life and it must not be pushed aside as a myth or a legend. The war, in all probability, was fought around 1000 BC, which marks the beginning of the Age of Kali *(Kaliyuga)* and the Age of Iron *(Lauha yuga)* in India. It is also not without reason that half a dozen wars that decided the fate of India were fought on the plains between Kurukshetra and Sonepat. In the seventh century AD Hieun Tsang visited the site the entire area was 'still covered with bones.'

Amongst the principal historical sites associated with the Mahabharata War mention may be made of Hastinapur (District Meerut, UP), where the Kauravas attempted to burn alive the Pandavas in a lac house; Bairata (ancient Viratanagar, District Jaipur, Rajasthan), where the Pandavas lived in exile; Panipat (ancient Paniprastha, Haryana); Baghpat (ancient Vrikshaprastha, District Meerut, UP); Indraprastha (Purana Quila, Delhi);

the five strategic villages on the Yamuna system, asked for by the Pandavas in case a war was to be averted; Kurukshetra (Haryana), where the battle was fought; Mathura (UP), wherefrom Krishna hailed; and so on.

The archaeological explorations and excavations have revealed an identical material culture in the lowest levels of all these sites which binds them together. This culture has been designated as 'Painted Greyware Culture' since it is characterized by a peculiar type of pottery which is grey in colour and which is painted.

Professor Sankalia has raised two very pertinent issues : they concern the weapons of the war and the nature of warfare. Broadly speaking, he is of the opinion that on both counts the so-called war was of a very primitive kind, resorting mainly to combat in which physical strength and personal valour counted much more than anything else. The weapons of war were of an extremely simple nature since the real sophisticated ones mentioned in the epic are absolutely mythical : their existence could not be proved either by archaeology or by sculptural representation or by actual specimens belonging even to the first millennium AD not to say of the earlier millennia. In this connection attention is drawn to the references which point to the use of chariots, projectiles, hurling weapons, siegecraft, armour, etc., in more or less the proportion they were used in the medieval period. The horses and the elephants were used in the eighteen-day war. Certainly, numerically their combined strength was much less than that of the foot-soldiers but that has always been the case in the past.

Further, what about the *chakravyuha*? Was it a myth? Was it of a very simple kind? Could we quote any example from history and ethnography both in which the 'tribal people' have been able to plan out a battle array like this for their warfare? Thirty years of serious study of these subjects have completely failed to give me any reference of this kind. My own feeling is that it was a very sophisticated type of planning and therefore, the Mahabharata warfare cannot be dubbed as 'tribal' or 'mythical'.

The Mahabharata War is called *Dharma Yudha* even though it was fought for political reasons. Evidences of *Kuta Yudha* are no doubt available but obviously not much of the Chanakyaniti or Machiavellian tactics were employed. A few instances of deceit like Yudhisthira's telling a lie or Bhima's hitting Duryodhana below the navel are exceptions and not the rule of the war. Intellectualism in planning the *chakravyuha* (and other *makara, pipilika, hastivyuhas* as well) and ethics in day-to-day warfare marked the Mahabharata as much as the personal valour of the heroes since the usual concept of a hero is that he is physically omnipotent. The combats between one hero and the other have necessarily been shown. Let us not be misled by such references in evaluating the nature of the Mahabharata War.

History is a very peculiar subject since at every stage of its writing a historian may be seen evaluating the past and while doing so, it has often been seen that inadvertently he has used some yardstick which is applicable either to the present or to the recent past or to some other time and situation but not to the time of actual happening of the event. Something of the kind seems to have happened in the case of accounts of the Mahabharata War also, even by renowned writers. I make a strong plea to guard against this tendency.

Now about the weapons of war. It has often been alleged that the bows and arrows were primitive weapons since these have been closely associated with prehistoric man or aboriginal tribes. It may, however, be pointed out that in India right from the Stone Age till AD 1857 when 'arrows were showered by the Indian rebels on the company soldiers', bows and arrows have been used. The standard of archery was very high in the age of the *Mahabharata* where several names for bow *(dhanu, kodanda, druna, chapa, sarasana)*; for an arrow *(isu, aramukha, naracha)*, quivers and braces are given. The blazing and flaming arrows, like the *naft* and *khadanga* of the Arabs, used in India in the tenth century AD were steeped in oil.

A bow was composed of a stout staff bent into a curved shape. Bamboo, cane, horn and wood were commonly used for staves. The *Ajagava* or *Pinaka* of Siva, the *Sarnga* of Vishnu and the personal bow of Krishna were made of horn; the *Gandiva* of Arjuna was of bamboo; while the *Vijaya* of Karna was forged out of metal. Three principal materials had been recommended, viz. iron, horn and wood, and each had been further divided into several categories. In the group of 'iron', gold, silver, copper, black iron and oily iron have been included. Among 'horns', the best ones were those of the buffalo, *Sarabha* (a Kashmiri animal) and stag.

The wood preferred were sandal, *shala, cane, kukubha, anjana* and bamboo. Nowhere in the pre-or protohistoric times were horn bows used and this 'horn bow', in all probability, was a link between the simple wooden or bamboo bows of prehistoric times and the composite bows of the historic times. The horns were bent the reverse way of the natural curve. In this manner the reflex bows were made. The 'primitive' people, in any part of the world, have never shown so much excellence. Then there were silk or cotton threads, sinews of deer, entrails of buffalo or goat and seasoned bamboo barks, employed for the bowstring.

Both the 'simple' bows, as represented on the obverse two groups of the punch-marked coins, having a curved stave and a straight string, and the composite' bows were known to the *Mahabharata* archers. The main constituents of a composite bow were threefold, viz. horn for the belly, wood or metal to give stiffness to the centre and sinew for the back. *Pinaka, Sarnga, Gandiva* and *Vijaya* were all composite.

Since highly finished horn bows or composite bows were expensive weapons and were used mainly by famous knights or royal princes, the bamboo and wooden bows, though less effective and used by common soldiers, have been extolled in the *Mahabharata.* Those used by the noted warriors were of nine *vitastas* (four and a half cubit) and the ones used by the common soldiers measured 96 *angulas* or four cubits. The horn hows were, however, shorter in length. The Pinaka and *Sarnga* measured three and a half cubits each. Thus, by and large, the bamboo and wooden bows used in the Great War were four and a half cubits long, the medium bows three and a half cubits, and the inferior bows only three cubits. The metal and horn bows, confined to the mobility, were shorter and stiffer measuring three to three and a half cubits. Metal and horn bows were made either of iron or horn separately or of the two substances conjointly. The horn bows were well shaped and often decked with gold and silver.

Ten types of arrowheads, namely *aramukha* (serrated), *ksurapra* (with a razor blade), *ardhachandra* (crescent-shaped), etc., have been mentioned and each was meant for a specific purpose. *Aramukha* was best suited for cutting strong object, *ksurpra* for cutting arrows of the enemy, *ardhachandra* for aiming at the throat and so on. *Isu* measured five span or three feet with a point of six inches. This tallies with the arrows represented in the Sanchi reliefs which appear to be a metre or a metre and a half in length. The shafts were made of *shara,* reed and bamboo which is clear from the term *vainara.*

Arjuna's arrows were made of reed and metal. Those made of iron and black iron have been referred to in the *Dronaparva*. The *Virataparva* describes the sharp-pointed arrows made wholly of metal and whetted on stone.

Arjuna killed an elephant with a stout *naracha* which penetrated the animal's body right through. The *Karnaparva* refers to *narachas* steeped in oil. They may have been lubricated to pierce surely and smoothly. The practice of inscribing names of figures on the arrowheads, as mentioned in the *Dronaparva,* continued throughout and in the Tanjore armoury a few inscribed arrowheads of the fifteenth-sixteenth century AD can still be seen. The *Dronaparva* again gives a list of forbidden weapons and mentions *inter alia* arrowheads made of monkey bone, cow bone, and elephant bone.

Poisoned arrows and those having ignited matter wrapped round the point were recommended only in an emergency and as a last resort. Arrows either too heavy or too light and those made of unseasoned reeds were prohibited from use. Similarly those with too wide a notch, a weak or crooked shaft or with imperfect points were prohibited. I have deliberately omitted the miracles performed by the archers or references to the arrows that produced fire, water and other distinctive elements such as serpents of various deadly forms, thinking them to be poetic fancy. After all, basically it is an epic. It may also be noted that the arrows have a continuous history in India. Anangapal fighting against Mahmud Ghazni (AD 1006), Hemu with Akbar (AD 1556), and Sadashiv Rao Bhau with Ahmed Shah Abdali (AD 1761) were all killed by arrows, shot by their adversaries.

Coming to spears and javelins we notice that spears and javelins excavated from the Indus sites are unaccountably primitive in form, thin and broad in the blade and without any strengthening mid-rib, except in one case from the upper levels of Mohenjodaro and with a tang instead of a socket. This was not the case with the examples in the *Mahabharata*. The epic spear was a superior weapon. *Shakti* or *mahashakti,* like modern *barachha,* was very sharp, made of iron and often oiled for smoothness. Some of them were enriched with an inlay of gold and beryl as well as studded with precious jewels. When used by the charioteers these were called *rathashakti*. According to the *Nitiprakashika*, a later work, *shakti*, on an average, was three to four cubits long with a triangular, quadrangular, pentagonal, hexagonal or even an octagonal blade. It was taken up and thrown with both hands and was utilized to serve six functions. This was used by the foot-soldiers.

Kunta was a lance, a kind of barbed dart, six to ten cubits long. It had an iron body, a pointed head and generally a hexagonal blade. *Nitiprakashika* refers to a *kunta,* like *shakti,* could also be manipulated in six ways. The same text prescribes that a person on an elephant should be assailed by an arrow and the one in a chariot by a *kunta*.

Prasa was seven cubits long and was made of red-coloured bamboo with a metallic head pointed at the fore-end. It was adorned with silken tufts. When hurled, it felled the enemy on the ground. It could be operated in four ways. *Prasas* were used by elephant-riders, horse-riders, charioteers and other mounted warriors.

Bhalla (modern *bhalla*) was a socketed weapon with a long blade and a bamboo shaft. The blade was border at the lower end, double-edged with or without medial rib and with a hollow shank into which the shaft was inserted. It was a thrusting weapon, used by foot-soldiers, operated with both hands and seldom hurled. On one of the lintels of *Stupa* at Sanchi, the scene of a besieged city is depicted, where the soldiers are attacking the enemy down with stones, arrows, swords and spears of *bhalla* category. *Shula* had an additional metallic piece, curved from the blade like an elephant-goad. In later sculptures it is depicted in the hands of Skanda or Karttikeya. Since the actual specimens of the *Mahabharata* period are not available these sculptural depictions of a later date can provide us a fairly good idea of the spears or javelins used in the Bharata war.

Mace, according to some scholars, is a weapon absolutely primitive in nature but then what about the club of Mahmud Ghazni with which he shattered the *linga* in Somanatha temple in AD 1025, or the ones used by the warriors of Timur the Lame, in AD 1339. The Mughal, Maratha and Sikh clubs of the sixteenth-eighteenth centuries are preserved in many Indian museums. Merely the existence of a kind of weapon or group of weapons, said to have been used only by the 'primitives', does not prove anything. As late as AD 1670 stone pebbles (*hat dhonda*) were used by the soldiers of Shivaji in the battle of Udaigiri.

In the Mahabharata War *gada* (club), a heavy weapon used in combat, had either round, oval, onion-like or pear-shaped (*sthulagara*) head. *Parigha*, of the same family, was studded with iron nails. In one place it is said to be hexagonal in shape, made of *ayasa* (iron) and four cubits in length. It can be compared with the Maratha *gurj* or Mughal *gargaj*. *Drughana* was a wooden mace. In the fourth century BC also the club was the chief weapon of the Sibi tribe. Plutarch says, 'In the capital of Malloi, Alexander received a blow on his neck from a club which forced him to lean for support against the wall, with his face towards the enemy.' It could be handled in twenty different ways such as bending, stooping low, springing forward, retreating, etc. The mace-fight was a highly developed art in the age of the *Mahabharata*. Exponents in this art were Balarama, Krishna, Salya, Duryodhana, Jarasandha, Bhima and others. The *Adiparva* narrates four kinds of *gadayudha*: (i) *praksepa* (in which the weapon was hurled at the enemy at a distance), (ii) *viksepa* (close fight at the weapon's end), (iii) *pariksepa* (brandishing it all around amidst the foes), and (iv) *abhiksepa* (hitting the opponent in front). The circling manoeuvres or *mandalas* (also called *marga*) associated with club-fighting are repeatedly mentioned in the *Adiparva*. The duel between Bhima and Duryodhana, in the *Salyaparva* provides us the vivid description of this fascinating fight; the entire repertoire of tricks is evident here.

Dagger was called *asiputrika* or *asidhenu*. Its other variety was *maustika*. The battle-axes have been mentioned under several names, such as *parasu, parasvavadha, kulisa* and *kuthara*. When it had two sharp blades, one on each side, like the Mughal *tabar* or Rajput *farasa*, it was called *pattisa*. Battle-axes, represented in the sculptures at Bharhut and Sanchi and also at places of later art, prove that this weapon of war has not undergone any significant change centuries after.

There were two kinds of *sataghnis* (literally 'the hundred killer'). The first was used by hand. It had the shape of a hammer and was studded with iron spikes. The other *sataghni* was a kind of instrument propelling stones. These were, as referred to in the *Shantiparva* and *Sabhaparva*, kept on the walls of fortresses in order that the stones might be thrown through them on a besieging force attempting an assault. These were provided with wheels to facilitate movement. Two stone-propelling machines called *Mahashilakantaka* and *Rathamusala*, were devised by Ajatshatru of Magadha in the sixth century BC.

Vajra (thunderbolt), *pasa* (noose), *chakra* (discus), various *yantras* and mythical weapons have been omitted here, because they cannot be corroborated with any archaeological or existing evidence. Their literary description or artistic representation on coins and in paintings and sculptures of subsequent period does not help us much.

The *Mahabharata* warrior put on clothes made of antelopes and other animals for their defence (*Bhismaparva*). The soldiers, according to the *Udyogaparva*, had the bracelets made of bull's hide. Warrior Kripa's arm, as mentioned in the *Bhismaparva*, was made of tiger's skin. Besides padded coats of quilted cotton, informs *Karnaparva*, the soldiers used *verman* (coat-of-mail) and *kavaca* (corselet or breast-plate), made of iron covered with lacquered ornamenation in gold and colours. *Sirastrana* (helment) finds mentioned in the *Karnaparva* and *Dronaparva*. The helmet of Duryodhana was a very formidable one (*Bhismaparva*). *Kanthathrana* of *Dronaparva* was a neck-protector and *kanchuka* was a jacket which extended upto the knee joints. *Nagodarika* was a glove to protect the fingers whose other variant, as discussed in the *Vanapara*, was *angulitrana*. The *hastaghna* (also called *hastavapa* in *Virataparva*) or *tolatra* was a bracer used by an archer to protect his arm from the blow of the string. Dronacharya, when wounded, raised his visor, and Arjuna took the opportunity to aim at his face, an arrow which proved fatal.

Horses were also covered. Frequently the words like *pithaka* (*Adiparva*), *pithamarada* (*Virataparva*), *khalina* (*Bhismaparva*), *asvastara, paristoma, rankava,* etc., have been used for the covering of a horse's back. These were, in all probability, varieties of saddle. *Kaksya* (girth), neck-chains, bells, wreaths, nets and umbrellas were equipments of elephants. The elephants with *howdahs* on their back and pendants on their front are depicted in the art of Bharhut and Sanchi.

Shield has been frequently mentioned in the *Bhismaparva* and other *parvas*. *Charma* was made of hide while *saravarna* and *sarovara* was of iron. *Phalaka* of the *Sauptikaparva* was a round shield with a convex surface similar to those found on the Indo-Greek coins, in the Gandhara sculptures or in the Ajanta paintings.

It was the age of the chariots although horses and elephantry were playing important roles. In the absence of metallic stirrups, not known then, the *Mahabharata* cavalier may not have effectively controlled the horse and operated the weapons from its back. It is, however, possible that the stirrups were made of some kind of textile as it is done even now in certain quarters. This was, in any case, the beginning of cavalry and elephantry in India. The elephants and horses were employed in war but not on a massive scale. This was possibly the transition phase, the charioteers giving way to the cavalry and elephantry.

The war-chariot (*sangramikaratha*) was a small-sized two-wheeled vehicle drawn by two horses, occasionally by three or even four. The body of the car was exceedingly light as it consisted of a wooden framework, fixed to an axle (*aksa*), fastened by cow-hide thongs. Both the solid wheels and spoked wheel (*ara*) were used. Besides the spokes, a wheel consisted of rim (*pair*), a telly (*pradhi*) and a nave (*nabhya*). The rim and the belly together constituted the tyre (*nemi*). Almost every part of the chariot *apaskara* (wheel), *upastha* (driver's seat), *yuga* (yoke), etc. has been defined. The royal chariots were richly embellished. Raised to its top, the chariot had a pennon which was the ensign of the knight. Though adept in the use of all sorts of weapons, the car-warrior preferred bows and arrows, *rathasakti* and other missiles.

Thus, the Bharata War was neither 'primitive' in nature nor confined only to the 'combats'. The combats did take place but it does not determine the entire nature of the war. In AD 1799 at Srirangapatana Tipu Sultan had a combat, amidst firearms, rockets and artillery shots, with General Baird. The soldiers were recruited, regularly trained and paid monthly. The army was divided into several units. Arsenals were maintained and workshops, for the repair, were opened. There were centres where the arms were forged. Military science formed part of the school curriculum and *dhanurdharas, mahadhanurdharas* and archaryas were employed to train and discipline knights in the making.

Charas and *dutas* were engaged for espionage; several tactics and strategies were employed and battle arrays (*vyuhas*) arranged. The army marched, more or less, in a disciplined manner and camped in *skandhavaras*. *Bheri, dundubhi, sarikha, pataka,* including the *Panchajanya* of Krishna, were the instruments to raise the spirit of the soldiers in march. Medical aid was given to the wounded and those killed were (in the evening of each day of battle when the war stopped till the sun rose again and the conch-shell was blown the next morning) cremated with all honour: the funeral attended by the relatives and foes alike. All these arrangements, ethics, organization, planning, operation, tactics, strategy, etc. could never have been employed on such a massive and dignified scale had the Kurus, the Pancalas and the Pandavas been primitive or had the Bharata War been only a 'family feud' – a chain of combats in which only bows and arrows and smashing weapons like clubs alone were used. It was not 'hit-and-run' or 'stab-and-go' but a regular war, well planned, well executed and well fought.

Major P Sensarma's *Kurukshetra War – A Military Study* published in 1975, was, despite certain limitations, a pioneering work, and Colonel G.D. Bakshi has made the best use of it in his book *The Indian Art of War : The Mahabharata Paradigm*. It is heartening that a person in uniform, having first-hand knowledge of modern war, its planning and operation, has analysed the most thought-provoking war of mankind, fought three thousand years ago. And he has done it with meticulous care and without pride and prejudice. This analysis is an attempt, a very successful one, to gain insight into those military aspects of the age-old Mahabharata War that have some relevance to modern Indian conditions. The essential make-up of the Indian military mind has to be thoroughly understood before the American, Soviet, British or German views on war are grafted. The epic *Mahabharata* has been analysed by Colonel Bakshi from a purely military point of view which is the brightest aspect of this research work. The *vyuha* concept of the Mahabharata War is the most revolutionary and characteristically Indian concept – peculiar to the Indian psyche and military genius. It is the author's contention that it holds a great deal of significance for the Indian army today specially in the field of mechanised operations. His comparison of Indian *vyuahs* with the Soviet battle arrays and German Laager is both fascinating and informative.

The study of war is no fiction reading. It calls for the concentration of the scientists to understand why a particular course of action adopted by a commander of a smaller force could succeed against an apparently formidable foe. It is by the constant study of the theory of science of war, old and new, that a soldier can attain professional competence since the opportunity of participating in actual war comes very rarely in his way. That is why the great commanders have always been serious students of military history. War offers an extremely fascinating study, however bloody it may be. Colonel Bakshi has done a great personal honour in asking me to write the Forword to this excellent monograph but more than that he has done a very great service to posterity by unravelling the principles of strategy and tactics of the Mahabharata War.

Prologue

The Quest for an Indian Strategic Culture

George Tanham created a storm in Indian military circles with his book "Indian Strategic Culture". Tanham essayed forth in quest of a primordial or historical Indian Strategic Culture. After much analysis, he concluded sadly that there was none. India lacked a tradition of focussed strategic military thought and analysis. There was no coherent military tradition that had come down from the ancient past. Some years later, Stephen Peter Rosen essayed forth on another scholarly analysis in his book "Societies and Military Power: India and its Armies". He too raised the issue of a "Primordial Strategic Military Culture" in India and marshaled an array of historical facts to conclude that ancient India (in specific Hindu and Buddhist India) lacked a tradition of Strategic thinking. He concluded that the size of the ancient Indian Armies was grossly and outlandishly exaggerated. He quoted military experts like Martin Van Creveld to highlight that given the state of land surface communications, command and control means and logistical infrastructure, it was impossible to focus armies of over 20,000 strength in a given battle area. Somewhat surprisingly Rosen contradicted this nugget of wisdom later in his book when he credited ancient Rome with Armies that numbered 240,000 (from a population base of just 2.75 million). This amounted to a total military mobilisation of some 9 percent of the Italian population. The Indo-Gangetic plain is one of the most fertile tracts in the world and one of the most densely populated. It is hard to discern why Rosen finds the testimony of Megasthenes and other Greek authors about Armies in ancient India that had reached peak strengths of over 600,000, so hard to accept.

In 1990, I had written my Book "Mahabharata: A Military Analysis". This was precisely to analyse whether this ancient Indian Epic represented that quintessential – primordial Strategic Culture of India. A decade later, I have now rewritten this book – quite firmly convinced that the Mahabharata indeed, is the primal source book of Indian military thought. It enunciates an attrition-oriented military Paradigm- that constituted our primal strategic culture. The Armies described in the Mahabharata largely defined the military organisational paradigm that was to remain constant in India till the 10th Century AD. It consisted of a four-limbed Army with Infantry, Cavalry, Chariots and Elephant Corps. The Chariots were the prize arm of the Mahabharata period. The first major transformation occurred with the shock of collision of this attrition oriented school of war with the mobility oriented Military Paradigm of the Greek civilisation. Alexander's invasion, in real terms was an extended border raid. Alexander never fought the major Indian military power of that era— the Nandas. However, it is evident that his well-drilled Greek Phalanxes and Cavalry had perfected a far more mobile paradigm of war. The ponderous, four-armed Indian Armies (comprising Infantry, Cavalry, Elephants and Chariots) were structured for major battles of attrition and annihilation, generally in a pre-designed and flat battle area (e.g. The flat plains of Kurukshetra or Panipat). The Chariots, the pride of the ancient Indian Armies, lacked cross-country mobility. They could move only along the roads and tracks and operate on firm and flat battlegrounds. They could not match the mobility of the Greek Cavalry that had transformed the horse into an efficient battle platform. The Greek invasion caused a civilisational upheaval in ancient India. Kautilya (or Chanakya— the man who laid the basis for the transformation of the Indian civilisational unity into a political unification of the Indian Sub-continent) closely analysed the Greek military organisation, and the reasons for its success against the border kingdoms of the sub-continent. India lacked a good gene pool of horses and unlike the Greeks (or the Mongols after them) had not been able to transform the horse into an effective fighting platform. The Indian Chariots were too slow and cumbersome in the kind of mobile operations that Alexander waged. Chanakya noted with interest however that the Indian war elephants had made a terrific impact on the Greek Army. Kautilya skillfully exploited the shock of the encounter with War elephants to weave excellent psychological warfare themes. He skillfully used spies and informants to spread rumours of thousands of war elephants in the ranks of the Nanda Army. The terror of this ponderous war beast was exaggerated and embellished with lurid tales of their strength and ferocity.

The first encounter with the elephants of Porus had left a terrific impact on the Greek soldiers. These rumours served to sow the seeds of panic. The tired and war weary Greek Army simply mutinied and refused to go any further. They were terrified by the prospect of facing thousands of War Elephants. Alexander's legendary oratory proved to be of no avail and he was forced to call off his Indian campaign and head for home. The Greek Army thereafter fought its way out along the course of the Indus and headed for the Sea. For the first time in the history of warfare, a world conquering army had been stopped in its tracks *merely on the strength of a superb Information Warfare Campaign* that exploited the shock effect of a new weapon system—the War Elephant.

From the Mahabharata to the Arthashastra therefore, marks the shift from the direct to the indirect approach in Indian strategic thought. The redoubtable Kautilya concluded that Chariots lacked the requisite cross-country mobility for a more mobile form of warfare as opposed to the attrition paradigm of the Mahabharata era. He, therefore, *changed the emphasis from Chariots to War Elephants and from Attrition to physical and psychological mobility*. The elephant was a huge beast and was capable of excellent cross-country mobility. With the howdha laden with archers and spear wielding warriors, it formed an excellent fighting platform that could beat the horsed Cavalry in terms of speed and reach. It's greatest asset however was its shock effect. Employed in the mass it could generate sheer terror in the opposing Army. It was also an excellent elevated platform for command and control. Elephants thereafter became the prize shock arm of the ancient Indian Armies and the role of the Chariot declined sharply. Infact a Sanskrit shloka said, "Where there are elephants, there is victory". The ancient Indian Armies thereafter transited from a four-armed architecture to a three-arm organisation minus the Chariots. This organisation was to remain constant till the Tenth Century A.D. when the Muslim invasions began. The Elephant went out of vogue with the introduction of gunpowder and explosives. What is noteworthy however is the fact that Chanakya's is the first and to date, one of the most brilliant Information Warfare campaigns in global military history. After all, it stopped a world conquering army in its tracks and forced it to turn back purely on the strength of a psy-tack or psychological attack alone. From the time of the Maurayas therefore, the elephant has become the liet motif of Indian combat power.

What is of vital import however is the issue of the existence or otherwise of a primordial or historic Indian strategic culture that has been raised by American scholars like Tanham and Rosen. It is indeed surprising that Indian scholars and historians have not taken up this very vital issue for wide-ranging debate and analysis. In his eminently readable book, "A Fire in the East", Paul Bracken writes, "*the persistent patterns in the way nations fight reflect their culture and historical traditions and deeply rooted attitudes that collectively make up their strategic culture*. These patterns provide insights that go beyond what can be learned just by comparing armaments and divisions".

The *Mahabharata* is a source book of Indian military thought and tradition. It is an index of civilizational development. It is the Indian Weltanschauung. No modern analysis of the Indian military ethos can be complete unless it delves into this source book. It is a vast and encyclopaedic text and deals with almost all topics under the sun (in addition to war). In fact its author Rishi Krishna Dwaipayan (Ved Vyasa) called it the fifth Veda. 'What is not here', he asserted about his epic, 'is nowhere'.

A military student therefore has to unravel his way through a vast, labyrinthine maze of philosophy, ethics, rituals, politics and issues of culture and morality, etc. to get to the kernel of military facts. The quest can become exasperating at times. One is tempted to leave this epic alone and concentrate more upon Kautilya's *Arthashastra*. The latter work is purely politico-military in character and deals specifically with statecraft. In seeking to make a comparison between the state of military art in the ancient civilizations of India and China, it would be much simpler to rely upon the *Arthashastra* as a standard Indian reference work. It makes more sense to compare this specialized text with Sun Tzu's magnum opus. Such an approach would lead to simplicity of treatment and facilitate a comparative analysis of the state of the art in ancient India and China.

However, in bypassing the *Mahabharata*, we would be omitting the pristine source of Indian military thought. Kautilya's *Arthashastra* repeatedly paraphrases the *Mahabharata* as the basic work of reference. Military details in Kautilya's text (*vyuhas*, administration, *Kuta Yudha*, espionage, etc.) are all largely paraphrased from this source book. A neglect of the *Mahabharata* therefore would mean bypassing the primary sources and concentrating upon the secondary source materials. To that extent an objective analysis of the military content of the *Mahabharata* epic is an essential and inescapable first step towards the study of ancient Indian military thought and traditions. Without such a reflective look back, it would not be possible for us to evolve any military doctrine that is Indian in essence and outlook. As a potential superpower, India owes it to herself to formulate an indigenous Indian military doctrine. To formulate such a doctrine of war it would be essential to carry out a study of our ancient military heritage first. Hence the importance of the *Mahabharata*. It has specifically been chosen for study over Kautilya's *Arthashastra* because of its immense popularity and hold over the Indian mind.

In this book, therefore, an attempt has been made to take an objective look at the military content of the *Mahabharata*. To lend objectivity to the analysis, an attempt has been made to view it in relation to the development of military art in a neighbouring civilisation of matching antiquity. Regular historians and academicians would definitely be more qualified to handle such a scholastic enterprise. However, they would lack the background of contemporary military thought and experience. This book seeks to fill this void, and hopes that the academics can then be prompted to conduct more specific research based on this backdrop.

The prime thrust of this book has been an attempt to gain insight into those military aspects of the *Mahabharata* that hold some relevance to modern Indian conditions or at least help us to understand the stages of evolution in Indian military thought and outlook. The epic has a surprising amount to offer in this direction. It provides a basic insight into the makings of the Indian military mind. The present Indian Armed Forces have a rich heritage and military tradition that dates back almost 5000 years. Today we need to formally study this tradition of soldiering.

Indian Military Psychology

Myth is the basis of reality. The *Mahabharata* is a significant military myth of the Indian people. It provides a very deep psychological insight into the makings of the Indian military mind. When we undertake such a study, we realize with a shock that the psychological attitudes are fixated – they are a racial constant. The major flaw in the Indian military make-up has been its chivalry and reliance upon the direct as opposed to the indirect approach in military strategy. The flaw is with us to this day. The British military connections only formalized this mindset.

The *Mahabharata* also highlights the strengths of the Indian military mind and its basic characteristics. Just as art forms are cultural constants, so also forms and patterns of warfighting become deeply ingrained in the collective psyche of a people. Forms of war that suit the innate genius of a people will always prove most successful.

Mao ZeDong's greatness as a military thinker lies precisely in this field. China is a vast and rugged country. Chinese folklore is full of the exploits of peasant rebellions against tyrannical warlords and dukes. As films of the Bruce Lee genre have adequately demonstrated, the Chinese folk hero is the peasant rebel. China is one of the most rugged and mountainous countries in the world. From times immemorial she has been the dream country of bandits and roving warlords. Chinese history is replete with countless uprisings, revolts by peasants and reigns of terror perpetuated by bandit hordes. In fact the first known guerilla war in history was fought there in 360 BC when Emperor Huang of the Han race defeated the Mao tribesmen of Tsi-Yao in a long-drawn war. Then there were the bandit hordes that terrorized China in the period of the Warring Kingdoms' (450-300 BC). Towards the end of the Tang dynasty in AD 875 we again hear of a Huang Chao and his roving rebel bands. The Ming dynasty was overthrown by a peasant revolt in 1628 led by Li-Chuang. The T'ai-p'ing rebellion of 1851 is a fact of fairly recent history. In fact the number of such instances that can be quoted would fill pages. The Chinese psyche seems to have a peculiar fascination for bandit- or irregular-style operations. Perhaps it is the influence of geography on the mental make-up of an entire people – but bandits and rebels have long been the folk heroes of the Chinese masses. They have been eulogized in their history, literature and ballads.

Mao ZeDong was born among the Chinese peasantry. From his earliest youth, his imagination was stirred by the tales of military heroism – both the triumphant wars of the past emperors and the feats of arms of the peasant rebels. In fact the main source from which he imbibed the military lore of his country are two romantic novels dealing with peasant uprisings. These are *Shui Hu Chuan* which has been translated by Pearl S Buck as *All Men are Brothers* (also called *Water Margin*), and *San Kuo*, translated by Brewitt Taylor as *The Romance of Three Kingdoms*. Mao read these as a small boy and they left a profound influence on his mind – an influence that surpasses even that of Sun Tzu.

Mao's genius lay in adapting the theory of People's Revolutionary Warfare to suit the innate genius of the Chinese people for guerilla warfare.

The style of warfighting that we choose for ourselves must suit the innate genius of our people. It must mesh with the pre-existing cultural context of their psychological imprinting. What is this cultural context? What is this military imprinting? The *Mahabharata* clearly provides deep insights. The salient factors that emerge are:

(*a*) *Large standing armies*. The Indian military tradition has relied upon large standing armies. India is primarily a civilizational entity. In her rare phases of political unity she has settled for large standing armies of an imperial nature. The Mauryan armies of Chandragupta and Ashoka were such armies. So were the armies of the imperial Guptas and later the Mughals. The British Indian Army of the Second World War at 2.5 million men was the largest volunteer army in world history. At 1.2 million men today, the Indian Army is the fourth largest in the world.

(*b*) *Vyuhas*. Indian armies from the *Mahabharata* period onwards have been combined arms forces. They had infantry, cavalry, chariots and elephants. These were trained to fight in well-known formations with setpiece battle drills called *vyuhas*. These will be the main object of study in this book.

(*c*) *Line versus the strongpoint*. The Great Wall of China at one stage signified the historical Han attitude towards defence – a vast defensive line, an endless wall to seal China from the barbarians. It is one of the wonders of the world as far as architectural excellence is concerned. It was one of the great historical failures as far as military effectiveness was concerned. The Indian defensive tradition has been centered round forts, the 'Garh' or 'Quila', the strongpoint that fights to the bitter end against a besieging army. The 'point' and not the 'line' therefore is the Indian military inheritance in defence. Yet India and Pakistan today have largely fallen back to the linear warfare philosophy of the First World War. Let us be certain that it goes violently against the very grain of the Indian military tradition – a tradition that is replete with the heroic sagas of famous forts, Chittorgarh, Shingarh, Chattisgarh and scores of others that dot the Indian landscape. It is in nodal points or 'admin boxes' of the Burma type (Second World War) that Indian troops will give their very best. The long, thin, red line is a historical invitation to disaster.

The Grand Battle

The entire thrust of Indian military history is towards a single, decisive battle that decides the fate of the vast reaches of the subcontinent. Whether it is the Mahbharata War on the plains of Kurukshetra, or the First, Second or Third Battle of Panipat very close by, the imprint is unmistakable. The Indian soldier is historically programmed to give his best in a short but decisive battle where all is staked and either won or lost in a single day. A short but intense war therefore suits the Indian psychological make-up. Long wars will lead to *vairagya*. This is something that our statesmen, generals and armchair strategists must take to heart.

To do this they will have to analytically examine the roots of the Indian military tradition. The essential make-up of the Indian military mind must be understood before we graft American, Soviet, British or German views of war on to this framework. This book then is a humble attempt to fill a long-standing void. A beginning has been made by studying the *Mahbharata* as a source of the Indian military heritage.

Studies in Indology

Beyond the Analysis of the *Mahabharata* from the purely military aspect, the study of this great Indian epic should constitute one of the major thrust areas of Indology. This magnificent epic is monumental in its sweep and grandeur. It presents a microcosm of the Indian civilisational context. Along with its subtext- the *Gita*, it provides an over-arching philosophy for the performance of action in a totally self-less manner. Guilt attaches to the personalised or individual ego. When an individual acts not from the standpoint of his limited self but for the good of his larger community, his country and his people- no guilt attaches to him (even if he kills another human being)

Gita : Ideological Basis for Fighting

The Gita thus provides one of the most coherent ideological basis for war-fighting that is as relevant today as it was some three thousand years ago. The military commanders' main objective in battle are to manage the two negative and disorganising emotions of *Fear* and *Guilt*. Both these emotions are disruptive of coherent thinking and action, and the greatest degraders of combat effectiveness and combat cohesion of units and armies. The Gita addresses these two facets directly. It propounds the ideology of a non-material basis of the human personality that survives the body. Such a deep-rooted conviction helps the soldier to withstand the fear of death, wounds and annihilation. The second facet that the Gita addresses is the facet of guilt. The Guilt of killing a human being can be profoundly debilitating. Arjuna faces the battlefield and sees his kinsmen arrayed against him. The thought of killing his rleatives, teachers and friends in war overwhelms him with guilt. This guilt renders him ineffective for combat. The Gita ideology thus directly addresses the key concern of the combat manager of today— how to overcome or manage the twin disorganising emotions of guilt and fear. Guilt, the Gita concludes, attaches to the individual ego. Guilt can not attach to an individual if he acts not from the stand point of the self— the narrow and selfish ego— but from the transpersonal stand point of performing his duty for his Country, his Regiment, his Unit. He thus places service before self. He places the higher and collective good above his individual goals and needs. This in itself activates the self-transcending class of emotions – (courage, altruism, sacrifice, patriotism) which alone can overcome the "self assertive" class of emotions like greed, lust, fear, selfishness etc.

Mahabharata : A Paradigm of Historical Patterns

Some years ago, Francis Fukuyama had popularized the concept of the "End of History". The triumph of the ideology of free market, capitalism and liberal Democracy over the totalarian ideology of Communism and Fascism he felt, signified the decisive end of a phase of historical evolution. The triumph of democracy was ultimate and final. There were no more ideological conflicts or wars left to be fought or won, he felt. History would henceforth become so dull and so boring. The concept of "Endism" created a stir in intellectual circles. However, history can not stand still or be frozen forever. Water must ceaselessly be in flow. Otherwise it stagnates and decays. Degeneration and rot set in. Change is a law of life. Today Samuel Huntingtons "Clash of Civilisations" has replaced Fukuyama's endism. The study of India as a civilisational entity therefore has acquired even greater significance. It is here that we find in the Mahabharata epic a veritable treasure house of civilisational myths and traditions. Strangely, these are not just relevant to the Indic civilisation but have a universal quality that transcends the civilisational fault lines. The Mahabharata has a message that is not just relevant to the Indian civilisational context but is relevant to the entire human race— especially at this critical juncture of crisis in the human condition. Some of these facets have been discussed in this book in detail. These are :-

(a) *Zeitgeist* : *Zeitgeist* is a German word that means the moral and ethical tone of an age. it is the contention of many Indologists and scholars that the moral and ethical tone of the Mahabharata is surprisingly similar to the Zeitgeist of our present Industrial Civilisation. The cardinal liet motifs are an emphasis on the self-assertive class of emotions of greed, selfishness, lust, avarice and envy. Unbridled competitiveness led to the two world wars in the 20th Century. "Greed is good" and "more is not enough" are the central credos of capitalism today. Hedonism is the primal cult of the Industrial civilisation. In the Mahabharata period, we see the Vedic pastoral society gradually transform itself into city-states on the Athenian model. These ancient cities were the foci of capital accumulation even then. Opulence, greed, covetousness, the lust for gold and voluptuous women, envy, jealousy, pride and hatred were the liet motifs of that age. Today we have a consumerist vision of society that is an ideological clone of the Zeitgeist of the Mahabharata— albeit on a colossal, global scale. The Industrial civilisation has uprooted almost half of mankind from the sylvan pastoral societies in the villages and packed them in cities, metropolises and slums. Today televised images fan greed and envy and power the engines of commerce in a consumerist society. It is a society in deep spiritual and ecological crisis. The similarity with the Zeitgeist of the Mahabharata is marked and astounding.

(b) *Endism : Expectations of an Epochal Conflict* : Mahabharata was an Armageddon, an Apocalyptic war that marked a "Yuganta" - the end of an age or an era. To that extent it has marked similarities with the philosophy of "Endism" propounded by Francis Fukuyama. Today the Industrial civilisation that is based on fossil fuels is coming to an end. It is based on the fossil fuels of coal, oil and natural gas. These resources are the carbon capital of this earth. These are being depleted today at an alarming pace. Oil will last at best for 40 years, natural gas for 70 years, coal for a 100 years. And what then? What happens to all this massive infrastructure of the oil based civilisation, the refineries, the cracking plants and pipelines, the oil tankers and trains, the oil fired thermal plants and powerhouses? That is only half of the problem. Reckless burning of fossil fuels is unfixing the Carbon (fixed by millions of years of evolution) from the earth's surface and subsurface back into the atmosphere. This could lead to global warming, the Greenhouse effect, the melting of the ice caps and another mythical flood or worse ecological catastrophes. Whichever way we look at it, we are nearing the end of one civilisational cycle. Hence the global relevance of the message of endism in the Mahabharata. A global cycle ends usually in a cataclysmic Armageddon. The Mahabharata was one such war. Are we headed for another Apocalypse?

Patterns of History and Change

The Mahabharata signifies the Indian concept of History as Cycles of Change. The patterns of history are cyclic and repeat themselves at regular intervals as it were. The essential pattern of events remains the same, only its form and details might differ. The Mahabharata was a civilisational Armageddon fought with bows, arrows, spears, maces, javelins and chariots, elephants and horses. Tanks, aeroplanes, missiles, precision guided munitions and even nuclear chemical and biological warfare weapons and information technology may now be used to fight a modern Armageddon. The Industrial civilisation is entering a terminal crisis. Unless it evolves beyond fossil fuels on its own (to Solar sails and Hydrogen fuel cells) it is headed for an ecological catastrophe. To save the earth, an Armageddon may put an earlier and swifter end to this Industrial madness of machines and metropolitan slums. Human history seems to swing between the emotional polarity of an ascendance of self-assertive emotions (lust, fear, greed, envy, jealousy, covetousness) and the opposite—self transcending class of emotions (Altruism, kindness and compassion, wonder, awe and reverence for all life forms). Are we headed today for the onset of a genuinely new civilisational order? A new human society that is clean and green? Massive changes in society can not occur in the absence of war and conflict. Will a new global and Green human civilisation have to be brought about by massive wars, Armageddons, and Apocalypses that will sweep away the old order to make way for the new? Are we inexorably gliding towards a Global Mahabharata? At the subcontinental level are we headed towards another regional Mahabharata with Pakistan? These are interesting pattern predictions that can be made on the basis of the Paradigm of change enunciated in the Mahabharata. It is therefore a myth with profound social dimensions.

The Indic Civilisational View of History

Let us be more specific. A deeper analysis of the Mahabharata (and its sub-text, the Gita) will show that these propound a very Indian view of history that seems to be an unintended synthesis of the Marxist and Arnold Toyenbees schools of History. Marxist schools place emphasis on the *forces of history* as the basis of all-historical evolution and change. Arnold Toynbees Western school laid stress on the *Individual* as the source of change- (the great emperor, the founder of an empire, the great captain of war, the charismatic leader) as the initiator of historical change. Thus the study of history is the study of Alexander and Napoleon, of Bismarck and Hitler, of Stalin, Roosevelt and Churchill, of Mao and Gandhi or Khoemeini and Castro or even Saddam Hussein. The great "spell binders" of history, these charismatic leaders are the prime agents of historical change. These leaders were only labels for the underlying Forces of History, aver the Marxist. It was only the Great Economic depression of the 1930s that enabled a man like Hitler to arise in Germany. In himself Hitler was unimportant. If not him it could have been Himmler or Goering or Haider or whoever.

The Avtara Theory

The Gita is a remarkable human document. Remarkable for its fascinating insights and practical wisdom. It was written by one of the most charismatic Indians who ever lived— the legendary Krishna who established a democratic Republican Clan of Yadavas in an era of absolute, hereditary monarchies. Krishna propounded the "Avtara" theory or the theory of "incarnation". "When Dharma or righteousness decline", he proclaimed "I incarnate to alleviate the suffering of the civilisation" (human condition?) Shorn of its religious context, does this assertion point to an Indian concept of history that is based on two primal parameters :-

(a) A decline in the human or civlisational condition (whenever Dharma declines....) that poses a condition of *challenge* from the social environment.

(b) The rise of charismatic civilisational leaders or icons in response to such an environmental challenge (Incarnate leaders – Incarnations of greatness).

The two facets are two sides of the same coin. The one can not arise without the other. Great Charismatic leaders arise only in response to great collective challenges from the environment. A great leader by himself would accomplish little in the absence of a collective civilisational challenge. Such a challenge in turn can not be overcome in the absence of such charismatic and inspired leadership. The central theme of the Mahabharata therefore is of surprising relevance to us even in this day and age. It has a core of wisdom that transcends the limited time period of the Epic itself and is of surprising relevance to the Industrial civilisation of today.

A Living Legend

As a military historian, let me in the end, come back to the original theme of this book, The Mahabharata epic deals with war. War is as relevant today as it was three millenniums ago. This is a sad reality that we must live with. War forms are a cultural constant even as art forms are a cultural constant. These primal forms tend to perpetuate and repeat themselves. The Mahabharata is not just a mythical tale. It is a living legend that has a surprising and tenacious hold upon our collective consciousness. Military leaders and managers of security must be fully aware of this cultural backdrop and context of soldiering in the subcontinent. The legend has a surprising relevance and continuity. India boasts of some of the finest fighting ethnicities that have proven themselves in combat in almost all the battlefields of the world against world class foes like the Germans, Japanese and Turks. These fighting ethnicities are today grouped in the Indian Regiments. The self same ethnicities (Dogras, Rajputs, Jats, Yadavas, Biharis, Assamese and even Nagas) are mentioned in the Mahabharata epic. The Dogras of today are the Dogratas (soldiers of the land of the two rivers) of the Mahabharata.

The Suryavanshi and Chandravanshi Rajputs (of the Solar and Lunar descent) are also eulogized in the Mahabharata. It speaks of the soldiers of Mathura (Jats, Yadavas, Ahirs), Shaubir, Angadesa and Kamrupa (Assam). The soldiers of Kamrupa were experts at handling war elephants. It also mentions Ghatotkach a Naga warrior. His mother was Hidimba after whom the modern Dimapur (Hidimbapur) is named. The modern Indian Military Academy (India's West Point) where the Army officers are trained is situated at Dehradun. The word Dehradun comes from the word "Dera-Drona" (the camp of Drona). Dronacharya, incidentally, was the great teacher who taught archery and the art of war to the Kauravas and Pandava princes. The historicity of Hastinapur (district Meerut), Bairota (ancient Virat Nagar District Jaipur, Rajasthan), Panipat (ancient Paniprastha, Haryana), Baghpat (ancient Vrikshprastha, District Meerut) and Indraprastha (Old fort, Delhi) are well established. So is Mathura a living city still. The Mahabharata is not just a fairy tale of gnomes and princes. It is a living legend. It is a core myth that lies at the basis of our psychological reality. It needs to be analysed in detail and studied in depth by scholars and soldiers alike. It has a great deal to teach us even today. *We need to turn to it precisely for the reason that generations of Chinese officers have turned to Sun Tzu's "Art of War"*. The wide scope of this epic however suggests that not just Indians but soldiers and scholars the world over need to focus on this epic to gain fresh insights. For in more ways than one, the myth of the Mahabharata reflects the Zeitgeist and reality of the post Industrial civilisation today.

In conclusion, I would like to place on record my gratitude to Major P Sensarma whose book *Kurukshetra War : A Military Study* has largely provided the inspiration for this work. I would also like to thank my dear wife, Sunita, who took time off from her busy household chores to type and edit this book.

1

Mahabharata : The Indian Weltanschauung

Myth, as the psychologists aver, is the basis of reality. The mythology of a people provides a deep insight into the collective psyche of that race. It possibly represents the collective 'script' that they are forced to act out repeatedly in various stages of their history. It defines their collective destiny. It is what the Germans call the Weltanschauung of the race. The word itself is not easily translated, but it represents the basic myth or 'the world view' of a people that dominates their collective psychological make-up. Racial myths are built around archetypal characters that have a tenacious hold upon the imaginations of all the men and women of that religious or cultural denomination. They represent a deep-seated undercurrent in the collective psyche, something that exerts an inexorable and tenacious influence. It is the primary basis of all cultural conditioning or imprinting.

All charismatic leaders and cultural revivalists have exhibited a very uncanny grasp of the mythology of their people. A deep insight into this racial or cultural mythology enables them to predict collective responses and harness deep-rooted emotions, prejudices and popular habits of thought for their own ends. The collective responses of a people to set situations can easily be predicted if we understand their basic myths. For the myth reveals how these people view themselves as an entity. Psychologists tell us that by the age of three or four each one of us finalizes his own basic 'script' of our lives. We are either born 'losers' or 'born to win'. The basic personality orientation is set firmly on that childhood script. The rest of our lives are spent in enacting or playing out that basic script in varied settings. Mythology is the basic script, acquired in the childhood of a race or a civilization. Its subconscious hold is even greater and more tenacious. It is an indelible cultural imprint.

To understand a people, therefore, one must understand their mythology. The *Ramayana* and the *Mahabharata* are the two great mythological epics of the Indian people. They provide a deep insight into the basic outlook and cultural imprinting of the Indian mind. We may debate their historicity, question their veracity and even their accuracy. We may contemptuously dismiss them as fairy tales but we cannot deny the indelible stamp that they have left upon the collective psyche of the Indian people.

In recent times we have witnessed an electronic revival of these ancient myths on Indian television. It has been something of a phenmenon. Sunday after Sunday, the *Mahabharata* and *Ramayana* serials have held millions spellbound. A peep into one's mythology is not only a peep into one's past but also an opportunity to peer deep into ourselves. The small screen therefore becomes a mirror into which the Indians have directed their gaze in fascination. The heroes that they see in action, the denizens that they perceive are primarily the creature shapes from the unconscious portions of their own collective minds. The moral tone of the *Ramayana* epic is lofty. It has led some Western writers to conclude that it is of later origin than the *Mahabharata*. The characters of the *Mahabharata* however are more human, more prey to the frailities of anger, envy, lust and greed, and overvaulting ambition. They seem more true to life. They represent a moral order in decay. It highlights the Indian world view. Evolution is not a strictly linear progression but is cyclical (or possibly sinuous). Civilization reaches an apogee of loftiness and superiority. Then it degenerates and slips into long periods of decline. Wars and pestilence wipe the slate clean and a new and a better order emerges upon the ashes of the old. Civilization re-emerges like a phoenix. That is the Indian world view.

Visions of Apocalypse

The *Mahabharata* represents Indian society in a state of decay. The *Mahabharata* is a tremendous vision of apocalypse. It is the Indian myth of a great Armageddon; a great, epoch-making war that destroys everything, that leaves humanity exhausted and spent. To that extent, the *Mahabharata* theme beautifully typifies the current decline in the human condition. The last century has already seen two apocalyptic world wars. It totters on the brink of a Third World War – a nuclear Armageddon that could wipe out all trace of life on this planet. To that extent the recital of the *Mahabharata* story, with its inexorable slide towards a self-destructive and suicidal conflict, its recital of all the unsuccessful diplomatic initiatives to prevent this final war, is spine chilling. Through the prism of the past, we can clearly see our present and possibly recognize our future. The *Mahabharata* myth talks of terrible weapons of war, the Brahmastra being the ultimate weapon. The mushroom cloud looms large over the world today. Thermonuclear destruction stares us in the face. In the wake of such a war we will face the ecological catastrophe of a nuclear winter. Even if the *Mahabharata* is a myth or a fairy tale, it is an awe-inspiring act of imagination. For it powerfully represents the reality of today; it painfully highlights the ills of the current human condition.

Was this war ever really fought? Or has all of South-east Asia been held in thrall by a mere fairy tale? British historians would, by and large, have us believe that the South Asian's *en masse* were afflicted by an overactive imagination. But the vivid imagery of the *Mahabharata* has left its indelible impress on the art and architectural forms of all South Asia. From the temples of India to Angkor Vat in Kampuchea, these mythical figures have been etched into stone and woven into the ballads and dance forms of India, Malaysia, Java, Sumatra and Bali. If it is all indeed a fairy tale, it is a remarkable and astounding tale to have so seized the imagination of millions upon millions of people for well over 2000 years.

These epics can be viewed at many levels – the purely historical, the civilizational, the artistic, the philosophical and the mystical. In essence both these epics represent the archetypal struggle between good and evil. What is remarkable is that good and evil are not regarded as pure black and white but as interminable shades of grey. At times it becomes difficult to differentiate between the two. Good, in trying to destroy evil, has to acquire all the characteristics of that evil. A socialist or a democratic state in trying to destroy a totalitarian state (like Hitler's) must acquire all the trappings of that coercive apparatus. Espionage, sabotage, subversion, assassination and disinformation must equally become its tools also. Only then can it survive and triumph. The distinction between good and evil remains very little in the ultimate analysis. Good and evil also join space and time as relative constructs of the human mind and not some universal constants or unalterable absolutes.

It is my contention that both the *Ramayana* and *Mahabharata* epics are woven around a kernel of historical truth. Poetic licence and exaggerations have blown it out of all proportion, but nevertheless, the core of historical and psychological truth is so strong that it continues to dominate the cultural landscape of the subcontinent even today.

Both these epics can be viewed at many levels of understanding: as history, art, philosophical speculations or even as sociological and anthropological data. In the main, they provide a deep insight into the essential psychological make-up of the Indian people. It is like the concentric ripples that appear around the spot where a stone has fallen into the water. Each concentric ripple expands our understanding and yet encompasses all that went before. The aim of this book is purely to analyse the *Mahabharata* myth from the military viewpoint. Since this myth holds the key to the Indian psychological make-up, it also contains the fountainhead of Indian military thought and attitudes. Well over 2000 years have passed but, as this analysis will show, little has changed in essence. The cultural conditioning of the Indian soldier has its roots deep in the *Mahabharata*. The philosophical inspirations for soldiering in India are still undeniably drawn from the *Bhagavad Gita*, a vital part of the *Mahabharata* myth.

Professionalism

The Indian philosophy of yoga places emphasis on skill in action. This has been the basis of the highly professional attitude of the Indian Army. Today the Indian Army is the fourth largest army in the world and amongst the most battle-tested. It fought with distinction in both the First and the Second World Wars. In the Second World War it had the distinction of being the largest all-volunteer force in the world. There was no conscription in India. Yet 2.5 million men volunteered to fight on the distant battlefields of Europe, Africa and South-east Asia. The basic well-springs of this highly professional attitude lie in the philosophy expounded in the *Mahabharata*. Skill in action and courage are virtues that are extolled as an *end* in themselves.

After Independence the Indian Army has fought four major wars and long-drawn counterinsurgency and anti-terrorist campaigns. Whereas in other Third World countries there have been a rash of coups and tinpot dictators, the Indian Army has stood firm by its apolitical traditions. The same has not happened in Pakistan. Perhaps the historical roots of it all lie in the psychological attitudes of professionalism and excellence that were nurtured in the *Mahabharata* epic. Courage is a way of life – for the Indian soldier imbibes the heroic tales of valour of Abhimanyu, Arjuna, Bhima and Karna from his very childhood.

Why did the Indian troops fight so well even for the British? The feats of courage and sacrifice of Indian soldiers have prompted Philip Mason to pose this question time and again. The psychological explanation for this comes from the professional attitudes of functional excellence ingrained in the *Mahabharata*. To the Indian soldier, skill in action has long been an end in itself. He gave his life in the First and Second World Wars not out of some mercenary zeal (he was hopelessly poor paid) but because the British realized his innate cultural conditioning for bravery in combat. The Indian soldier's deeply ingrained sense of honour or *izzat* and of being true to his salt can be traced back directly to Bhishma's and Dronacharya's decision to fight for Duryodhana regardless of personal predilections. To them Duryodhana personified the state of Hastinapur and they would be loyal to their salt come what may. The Indian soldier has always been excellent fighting material. To understand why, we must understand the myth of the *Mahabharata*.

In this book I have tried to analyse the epic from a purely military point of view. It is amazing to see that there are so many insights and lessons that hold a lot of relevance even in this day and age. The epic is immortal. Its basic tenets and guidance are equally applicable to soldiering in the twenty-first century. It is the source book of all ancient Indian military thought. The roots of the Indian military tradition can correctly be traced to this epic. The Indian military ethos has germinated from this ancient period of our history. The surprising fact however is the degree of its relevance even in this day and age.

2

Mahabharata : An Ideological Analysis

Krishna: Harbinger of Democracy

An essential feature of the *Mahabharata* myth is the story of Krishna. Krishna is elevated to divinity. He is extolled as an incarnation of Vishnu, the preserver of the Hindu pantheon. We know little today of the historic Krishna, except that he was a highly charismatic leader. His charisma was so unbounded that to this day it exerts a powerful influence upon the day-to-day lives of Indians.

Historians, therefore, would do well to study Krishna as a leadership phenomenon. There is a school of thought which contends that Krishna was a historic leader who first actualized the political concept of democracy in India. Krishna was not a hereditary ruler. He was spontaneously chosen as the leader of the Yadava clan. The Gopas (or the cowherds) of the Yamuna region made him their uncrowned king. A democratic form of government therefore flourished in parts of India almost 2500 years ago under Krishna. DR Parekh in his book *Krishna: Myth or Reality* writes thus about the Yadavas:

> "The Yadava clan to which Krishna belonged had sprung from Yadu, the son fo emperor Yayati and his Brahmin queen Devayani. They were a virile and pastoral people who were settled in the Vajra Bhoomi, the lush and fertile valley of the Yamuna river. Legend has it that they had developed a republican form of government in sharp contrast to the absolute, despotic and hereditary monarchies prevailing in the rest of the country. They selected their leader by consensus."

If we analyse the myth of Krishna, it appears that one Kamsa had staged a palace coup and deposed Ugrasen, the Yadava ruler of Mathura. Kamsa had enforced a tyrannical dictatorship. He had strengthened his position by marrying Asti and Prapti, both princesses of Magadha, the powerful kingdom of East India. He had visions of establishing a hereditary monarchy in the Yadava realm and set about it in a ruthless fashion. He was overthrown by the young Krishna, who reinstated democracy and ended the nightmare rule of the oppressor Kamsa.

The rise of Krishna and the rudimentary republican form of government must have posed a great threat to the established ruling dynasties of India. The Eastern 'confederacy' comprising the kingdoms of Magadha (modern Bihar) and Angadesha (Bengal) along with those of Chedi, Karush, Paundra and Vidarbha were alarmed by the rise of Krishna. The overthrow and killing of Kamsa, a hereditary ruler who had marriage ties with the mighty Magadhan kingdom, filled them with misgivings. The rise of republican rule in the Indian heartland must have had the same impact that the French Revolution later had in Europe. The ruling dynasties were alarmed. The fate that had befallen Kamsa could easily overtake them. The republican challenge had to be nipped in the bud.

Just as the European monarchies had ganged up against France in the seventheenth century, a similar variation of this theme could possibly have occurred in India in the times of Krishna. The rise of Krishna therefore symbolizes the first upsurge of democracy in this country and possibly in the world. This gives us an altogether different historical standpoint of viewing the *Mahabharata* as the story of the clash of two political ideologies – the nascent democratic ideal as embodied in the Yadava republics and the hereditary, despotic and absolute monarchial political systems then prevalent in the rest of India. The great hold of the Krishna legend now becomes easier to understand. We can easily compare its emotive fall-out with the tremendous upsurge of the more recent French Revolution. The charisma of India's first democratically elected/chosen leader has survived to this day. In deitifying Krishna the Indian people have intrinsically shown their great historical leanings for the democratic form of government. Democracy obviously is not a foreign transplant in Indian soil.

The Eastern confederacy of powerful kings now began a series of attacks on Mathura, the capital of the Yadava republic. Legend has it that Jarasandha, the powerful ruler of Magadha, attacked it 18 times. It is here that Krishna proved to be a master strategist. Mao Zedong in his military writings has almost made a fetish of tactical retreat. Such a retreat preserves the guerilla army. It induces the enemy to make mistakes which the defender can then exploit. Only by loss, says Mao, can loss be avoided. Unless a man parts with some money, he cannot buy goods. Tactical retreat is therefore a valuable military gambit. However, retreat was looked upon with great horrer in ancient India. It was the ultimate disgrace. Krishna boldly made a fetish of retreat even as Mao was to do 2500 years later. Krishna was then called 'Ranachod' (one who fled the field of battle). Krishna propagated that there was no stigma in retreat. It was a natural stratagem of war – essential to preserve one's armed strength. He did not subscribe to the 'Direct Approach' in strategy – that glorified suicidal battles. An unfavourable engagement must be broken off. Only that way can a commander ensure final victory. Krishna was the first Indian patron of what BH Liddell Hart has called the 'Indirect Approach' in strategy.

The Great Migration

Based upon the advice of the sage Parashurama, Krishna led his Yadava clans in a great strategic retreat that must rank even higher than the 'Long March' of the Chinese communists. The Yadavas left the Yamuna river plains, marched across the Rajasthan desert and settled down in Dwarka (modern-day Gujarat). Here Krishna built a great fort city looking upon the sea which was to become a great centre of commerce and trade. The withdrawal of Krishna from the central Indian heartland of the Indo-Gangetic plains saved his infant republic from the combined onslaughts of the monarchial powers led by the powerful kingdom of Magadha.

Krishna: The Grand Strategist

His exodus to the coastal belt did not marginalize Krishna from the power-politics of the subcontinent. Krishna proved his ability as a statesman par excellence by now using his diplomatic skills to ensure that the Yadava republic attained a position of pre-eminence in India. He allied himself with the powerful Pandava kingdom and used this alliance to overthrow the mighty Jarasandha, his old enemy of Magadha. One school of thought holds that Krishna then engineered events that would lead the Pandavas and Kauravas to engage in the war of the *Mahabharata*. This Indian apocalypse destroyed the power of the Indian heartland kingdoms.

Legend has it that it was a mighty war – an Armageddon that destroyed the political balance of the subcontinent. It created a power vacuum into which the Yadavas moved easily and naturally. As a piece of ruthless and cold-blooded statecraft, this feat has no parallels. It bespeaks a level of political sophistication that is hard to ascribe to those ancient times. Even if the *Mahabharata* is treated as a work of fiction, we must understand that literature mirrors the level of societal development. If Vyasa could visualise such an epochal conflict and the highly sophisticated power-politics of the sub-continental region, it highlights a very high stage of civilizational development.

The republican theme is not as far-fetched as it might appear on first hearing. It is a historical fact that there were republics in India in the times of the Buddha. The republican democratic form of government had originated much earlier and the name of Krishna is most closely associated with this early Indian 'movement for democracy'. This is the basis of the Krishna legend.

Krishna: The Philosopher

Even the historic Krishna, shorn of all the legends and poetic exaggerations, nevertheless emerges as a many-splendoured personality. He is a many-sided genius. So great are his accomplishments in diverse fields that some historians assume that there was not one Krishna, but several different personalities who are lumped under that one generic name today. Historical distance has blurred the individual identities and what emerges perhaps is a historic Krishna – a great general and accomplished warrior, a great statesman and a great philosopher – a man of action and deep reflection. The level of accomplishment in each of these diverse fields is of such a high order that it is difficult to believe that one single personage could have combined them all in his person. Krishna symbolizes Plato's ideal of the philosopher-king.

Gita: The Pursuit of Excellence

A great sub-section of the *Mahabharata* is the *Gita* – Krishna's exposition of the Doctrine of Desireless Action. It has become more famous than the parent epic itself. It is a work of great synthesis for it synthesizes the six schools of Indian philosophy (Yoga, Sankhya, Vedanta, Agama, Nigama, Nyaya). It provides an excellent ideological basis for fighting. 'Skill in action,' avers Krishna 'is Yoga'. The pursuit of excellence is an end in itself. It is its own reward. Krishna advocates action for the sake of action: to perform ones duty without seeking any reward or recompense.

The Indian Army was deemed the ultimate mercenary army when it served British imperial interests in the two world wars. At 2.5 million men, India fielded the largest all-volunteer force in the history of the world during the Second World War. Military pundits still marvel at the motivational basis that led Indians to lay down their lives in such distant battlefields. Historians like Philip Mason (*A Matter of Honour*) and Stephen P Cohen (*The Indian Army*) have tried to unravel the mainsprings of the combat motivations of the British Indian Army. The native sepoy's feats of courage were astounding. 'Men may come to the colours for pay,' wrote Mason 'but it is not for the pay alone that they win the Victoria Cross.' Several Indians won the Victoria Cross in the service of British interests, many thousands more laid down their lives. It amazes the historian. Mason sought answers in the Indian concept of *izzat* of the 'Quam' (sub-nationality) and the 'Paltan' (regiment).

A deeper philosophical source that he omitted to analyse completely is the ancient tradition of professional excellence that can be traced back to the *Mahabharata*. Even the Indian caste system in its extreme form can be viewed as a genetic quest for such professional excellence. The profession as a way of life ensured the genetic and environmental imprinting for excellence. The ideological basis for his military motivation is to be found in the *Gita*.

The *Gita* extols death in battle as the highest path to liberation. It preaches the immortality of the *'Atman'* that transcends the body (weapons cleave him not, nor the fire can burn). The Atman discards worn-out bodies like we discard old clothes. *'Na Hanyate – Hanyamane Sharire'* – it does not die with the death of the body. The *Gita* expounds the indestructability of the human personality which transcends the physical existence. It is this which gives spiritual solace to a soldier facing death and wounds in battle. Death in battle is a matter of honour indeed – it is extolled as the surest gateway to heaven or to salvation. To overcome one's deeply ingrained physical fear of death is also a form of yoga. Fear is the greatest fetter: one who casts off fear is truly free. The state of mind of the sage is the state of mind of the warrior.

Hence, in India there has always been a symbiotic relationship between saints and soldiers – a deep religious connection that is specially highlighted in the Sikh faith. The Sikh *gurus* raised an army of 'Sant-Siphais' (soldier-saints) to overthrow the tyranny of Aurangzeb. Shivaji, the great military leader of the Marathas, also laid considerable stress upon an ethical-spartan code of conduct for the soldier. Under the moral influence of his mother, Shivaji was almost a saint of sorts to the masses.

The Indian civilization, unlike the Chinese, has given a place of great honour to the soldier. In the Hindu caste hierarchy, the soldier (Kshatriya) ranks next only to the intellectual (Brahmin). In war he has a royal short-cut to ultimate liberation. In overcoming his fear of death and extinction, he becomes canonized into sainthood. He is enshrined in ballad and legend. He may or may not achieve salvation, but he does become immortal through public acclaim. The value system of ancient Indian society has always revered the courageous soldier and nurtured the tradition of bravery and sacrifice.

The basis of Indian military professionalism however may be traced to the quest for skill in action propounded by Krishna to the great warrior Arjuna in the *Gita*. The *Gita* is the only book written by a soldier, for a soldier, which yet has a wider universal appeal. It is an ideology woven around an unending pursuit for excellence – where excellence is an end in itself and serves as its own reward.

It is this deep cultural imprinting that lay at the basis of the sacrifices made by the British Indian Army and later by the Army of free India. The *Gita* provides one of the most coherent ideological bases for war. It provides a value system that overcomes the stresses of battle. The quest for perfection is an end in itself. It goes beyond religious tenets and applies to all professionals everywhere.

Fear and guilt are the main disorganising emotions that a Commander has to manage on the battlefield. The *Gita* tells us how to overcome fear— by declaring that the core of the human personality is indestructible and death is not an end, just an intergennum. The *Gita* also tells us how to overcome Guilt— the powerful emotion of guilt at killing another human being. This can be very debilitating. In fact the *Gita* begins with the scene of despondency into which the great warrior Arjuna has slunk out of guilt. Guilt attaches to the individual ego. Therefore do not act from the standpoint of the narrow and personal ego. Act in a selfless manner—as an instrument for a higher cause—for one's country and one's people. No guilt attaches to the person in that case. I am not the doer of these actions. My duty is a higher calling. Combat mangers even today would be hard put to devise a more rational ideology for combat motivations.

3

Incarnation : An Indian View of History

The Indians have often been accused of having no sense of history. The Indian concept of history seems to bear no passion for accuracy of detail or for chronology. The Indian concepts of time are relative and cyclical and there is a penchant for juggling astronomical figures. Despite this, the Indian people have displayed a passion for preserving certain aspects of their cultural history.

The Vedas, for instance, were handed down from generation to generation in an oral form by Brahmin families who were charged with their memorization. They were recorded in the written form by Ved Vyasa (who is also the author of the *Mahabharata*) almost 2500 years ago. The Vedas, the true source books of Indian philosophy, are with us even today. It is truly an astounding feat of racial memory. The encyclopaedic epics of the *Ramayana* and *Mahabharata* and the *Puranas* are further records of history as the Indians view it.

This history has however been recorded by poet-philosophers who have made full use of poetic licence to exaggerate, embellish and blow the kernel of historic fact into an outsized myth. That possibly was the only way it could have been preserved over the centuries. Each subsequent rendition has enlarged and added to the basic book. The first recension of the *Mahabharata* (called Jaya) for instance is said to have only 8000 *shlokas* (verses). The second recension had 24,000 *shlokas*, and by the third recension it had swollen to a staggering 100,000 *shlokas*.

One classic Indian technique of communication was the highly developed art of teaching by anecdotes. The *Panchatantras*, the *Jatakas* and the Hindu,

Jain and Buddhist mythologies incorporate many such anecdotal stories with a philosophical message. Such stories add to the length and historical inaccuracies of Indian myths. The same is not true of the purely philosophical texts like the *Yogasutras*, the *Gita* and the *Upanishads*. These are very brief, very pithy and a lot of meaning has been compressed into each single verse which is open to diverse interpretations. Each verse could inspire many volumes of commentary. It is obvious therefore that strict economy of words was exercised in transmitting philosophy.

On the other hand, myth building had been developed into a fine art. The anecdotal style was designed to capture the popular imagination. Exaggerations and poetic embellishments were intended to ensure that the story would survive the ravages of time. It is not difficult for the discerning to identify the core of historical fact in the myth. The only danger is that with the passage of time, so much is interpolated that the myth obscures the reality like weeds. However, we must remember that Indians have used history in order to philosophize, in order to abstract truths of a universal nature. The emphasis has been on the general and not the particular.

There are two basic schools of history today, the Arnold Toynbee school of Western historians and the Marxist school of history. The Western school has laid emphasis on the individual – on the great emperors or warlords who left an indelible impact on history, who moulded events and shaped the destinies of mankind. The Marxist viewpoint has downplayed the individual and stressed the forces of history – the socio-economic undercurrents which constitute the tides of history. These forces of history shape the flow of events. Individual leaders are incidental. They are merely labels for historical phenomena. Had it not been Hitler, some other cultural revivalist warlord would have appeared in his place in Germany. The real causes of the Second World War lay in the socio-economic factors unleashed by the great economic depression of the 1930s, the intense frustration generated by the economic collapse and the humiliation of the Treaty of Versailles. All these fuelled the Second World War. It was inevitable. Hitler was not its cause – he was only the symptom. It is surprising to note that the Indian viewpoint of history represents a curious synthesis of these two divergent schools of historical interpretation. This sounds a surprising statement but a little reflection will show that it is wholly true.

The Indian attitude to the interpretation of history is summarized in the famous verse of the *Gita* where Krishna declares to Arjuna, *'Yada-yada hi*

Dharmasya – Glanir bhavati Bharata, Abhyutt hanam adharmasya tadat manam sriyamyaham' (*Gita* Chapter 4, verse 7). This verse encapsulates the basic theory of Avatarahood. It says: 'Whenever righteousness (*Dharma*) declines, I incarnate to alleviate the crisis in the human condition.'

In the Indian view therefore history is shaped by two factors – a general condition of decline in human affairs, a condition of crisis or challenge from the natural or social environment and the emergence of a great leader or a cultural revivalist. Both these are two sides of the same coin. The one is not complete without the other. The condition of challenge is one half of the equation. The emergence of a great leader is its other half. In the absence of such a condition of crisis, it is difficult for a great leader to capture the imagination of the people. He incarnates or emerges to show a way out. He is a being with boundless charisma. He is an ideologue who simplifies complex issues. The *Avatara* is such a being. He has boundless charisma – the multitudes follow him blindly. He is a cultural revivalist who upholds the eternal law (the *Dharma*). He is primarily an ideologue who guides his people.

Vishnu is the preserver of the Indian pantheon. The concept of the incarnation of Vishnu is most interesting. There are nine known incarnations with a tenth yet to come. The incarnations follow a curious progression up the evolutionary ladder from fish, to amphibian, to mammal, to primate and then to full human form. JBS Haldane, the evolutionist, had noted this Darwanian progression several decades ago. Parashurama was the sixth incarnation of Vishnu. He lived well beyond his times and was around in the times of Rama, the seventh, and Krishna, the eighth incarnation of Vishnu. So it is obvious that the 'Avataric consciousness' is not confined to one being at a time.

The Vishnu consciousness is the revivalist consciousness – it is not confined to a single individual but acts, as it were, through a host of people who are so awakened or equipped. The person in whom this revivalist urge manifests at its peak is extolled as the incarnation of Vishnu. He examplifies the spirit of the age.

Incidentally, the Buddha is regarded as the ninth incarnation of Vishnu. He had that tremendous charisma, the diagnostic abilities to identify the ills of the human condition. He prescribed a simple, universal philosophy to overcome suffering. The icon of the Buddha has left an indelible stamp not only on India but upon the whole of Asia. The historical Buddha accurately personifies what the *Avatara* is meant to be – a being of boundless charisma who grips the popular imagination for generations.

The tenth incarnation of Vishnu which is yet to come is supposed to be the 'Kalki Avatara' – a great warlord who will destroy the present 'Kaliyuga' or industrial age and usher in the dawn of a new civilization that will be perhaps more ecological in its outlook. Very interestingly, these predictions seem to match those of Nostradamus who has forecast about a third 'anti-Christ' who will arise in the East. The historical veracity of these legends may be doubtful – but we all know that Nazi and Allied propaganda machines in the Second World War had tried to exploit the prophecies of Nostradamus for their own ends. The propagandists realized the tremendous hold that such myths have on the collective mind.

The *Avatara* theory is a peculiarly Indian conception. It provides an Indian viewpoint of history which predicts the rise of a great charismatic leader whenever the Indian civilization faces a crucial challenge from the social or cultural environment. Whenever the Indian polity goes into decline a great being will always arise – a great revivalist whom the people would treat as a God. He will usher in a civilizational renewal. He would be superhuman in his abilities – he will be Vishnu incarnate. Such is the strong belief of the Indian people. Krishna was possibly such a leader. He established a democratic order at a time when autocratic, despotic, and absolute monarchies were ruling in various parts of India. He was a great statesman who engineered a terrible war – a war that destroyed the despots and paved the way for the rise of his republican clans. He had a hypnotic influence on the people, the extent of which can easily be understood when we compare it with the euphoria generated by the French Revolution in Europe much later.

'Vishnu' therefore personifies a civilizational revival or a renewal of lost vitality; a restoration of the moral and ethical basis of civilization. He initiates a reinterpretation of the established tradition to meet the requirements of the changing times. His coming represents a renewal of the Indian civilization. Far more than a political entity, India is a great civilizational entity that has survived intact for over 5000 years. Its survival has been ensured by such revivalist leaders who arose in conditions of great environmental challenge. The revivalists and the innate popular yearning for such a revival are a symbiotic phenomena. They form a self-reinforcing loop. A condition of societal crisis demands the emergence of such a leader – a great leader slips into this slot. He fills the vacuum and dispels the gloom.

4

Notes on Chronology : A National Epic

The chronology of the *Mahabharata* and its accurate dating are deliberately being kept beyond the purview of this book. The prime aim is to analyse the military content of the *Mahabharata*. This will give us an insight into the evolution of Indian military thought and tradition. To that extent an accurate dating of the epic would add or subtract little from such an analysis of the state of military art.

The issue of dating the epic is controversial and the author would not like to venture into this historical minefield. However, even for purposes of a military analysis, one cannot altogether escape the need for viewing the thought content against the backdrop of a historical timeframe of reference. If we are able to fix a time slot we can then analyse it from the viewpoint of the development of weapon technology, military theory, and metallurgical aspects.

Above all, the best way of analysing the military wisdom of this epic is to compare it with a historical work of comparable antiquity. The best example that comes to mind is Sun Tzu's epic *The Art of War*. This will enable us to view the stages of civilizational and military development in India and China. A comparative analysis of the early military development in these two great civilizations would help us to gain useful insights into the epic and assess its value accurately. India and China are the world's oldest living civilizations. These ancient cultures that flourished in the fertile river valleys of China and the Indian subcontinent have more or less survived intact in their essential form for almost 5000 years. A comparison of the military art of India and China, as an index of the state of civilizational development in these ancient countries, would therefore help us to assess the *Mahabharata* epic in a more scientific way.

To attempt this, one would have to roughly ascertain the antiquity of the *Mahabharata* epic. Many Western Indologists have dismissed the *Mahabharata* as a myth with no basis in reality whatsoever or a war song of a petty family feud blown out of all proportion. This 'Western' school has its Indian adherents too. In fact, even as late as 14 September 1975 Dr DC Sircar (former Chief Epigraphist to the Government of India) declared emphatically that the *Mahabharata* was a myth devoid of any historicity. However, Doctors Pande and Gupta have done commendable work to establish the historicity of this war based upon archaeological and other evidence. A most laudable effort in this field recently has been that of Major P Sensarma (which has served as the source material for much of this book). Before the advent of Western (British) Indologists, the Mahabharata War was accepted as fact by almost the whole of South-east Asia and as such found a rightful place in its art, architecture, sculpture, painting, dance and drama.

Chronology

The notable stalwarts of chronology amongst Western Indologists are Max Muller, Pargiter and Roy Choudhary. They have generally placed the *Mahabharata* date around 950 BC. However, Mr. SB Roy (Director, Institute of Chronology) has, in his book *Date of Mahabharata Battle*, placed it between 1500 and 1400 BC, perhaps 1424 BC. SB Roy, based upon metallurgical evidence (use of iron and copper), dates it as 1400 BC. Of late another attempt was made to date the *Mahabharata* based upon astrological evidence and this has worked out as 1414 BC.

Archaeological Evidence

The *Puranas* mention that when Hastinapur was destroyed by floods the capital was shifted to Kausambi. Archaeologists have identified the scar left by the Ganga on some settlements. The period 800 BC has been roughly identified as that in which the capital was shifted. As this took place, according to the *Puranas*, five generations after the Mahabharata War, the events in the epic are to be placed in the ninth century BC.

The *Mahabharata* sites are historically authentic. The Hastinapur of the epic is the place of the same name in Meerut district. After exile, the Pandavas asked to be given just five villages: Paniprastha (Panipat), Sonaprastha (Sonepat), Tilaprastha (Tilpat), Vrikshaprastha (Bhagpat), and Indraprastha (the site where the Purana Quila was later built in Delhi). Kampiliya is the same as Kampil in Farukhabad district, and the identity of Kurukshetra is of course well-known. Archaeological excavations at these sites, particularly Hastinapur, have yielded objects which can be classified into five periods ranging from the pre-*Mahabharata* times to the medieval period. Excavations at Hastinapur and other sites have turned up evidence of an economy largely based on agriculture and livestock rather than trade and commerce. Herman Kulke and Dietmar Rothermund have pointed out that recent archaeological research has shown that all important places connected with the epic were all characterised by significant finds of painted Grey ware. This type of ceramics was produced in the period from 800 to 400 BC and in some places it could even be dated back to 1000 BC. Painted Grey ware is now widely accepted as an indicator of Aryan settlement. Perhaps the most interesting discovery is that of a dice from Ropar in Punjab. The dice is oblong in shape, made probably of ivory and bears the marking of one opposite three and two opposite four. This shows the popularity of the game of Chaupar (Chausar?) which dramatically changed the course of events in this epic.

The two historical views on dating the *Mahabharata* therefore place it at either 1400 BC or 900 BC. The latter date appears closer to the truth as it is substantiated better by archaeological evidence. However, considerable work is still to be done before a definite conclusion can be drawn.

In recent times scholars like Dr. D.N. Jha and others have spoken of the two stages of the Aryan or Vedic civilisation in ancient India. The Early Vedic age extends from 2000 BC to 1000 BC. Jha and others feel that the Aryans were basically a pastoral people and the political organisation was tribal. It was only towards the end of this phase that the Aryans switched from pastoral nomadism to settled agriculture. This led to the rise of the territorial state. We hear of the establishment of a series of agricultural settlements called Janapadas. In the second stage of the Vedic civilisation these territorial entities became larger in size and scale. Great cities were founded and agriculture flourished and generated a considerable surplus. These cities became the foci of capital accumulation and later the centres of trade, commerce, artisan guilds and ceramic industry, weaving of textiles and centre of learning. This period lasted from 1000 BC to 600 BC. The Mahabharata war then occurred in this second stage of the Vedic civilisation when it had crystallised into territorial state entities and city-states. In fact many of these states grew to respectable size and were called Mahajanapadas. The Mahabharata war was a war of the antagonistic coalitions of all these states. The ideological conflict in the ancient times was one between the hereditory monarchial system and the tribal clan or Republican system of government.

A 'National' Epic

Sister Nivedita in her eminently readable book *Footfalls in Indian History* has made some interesting observations. She says,

> "In Hindu literature there is no second work which can be called "national" in the same sense as the Mahabharata. The reader is at once struck by two features: in the first place its unity in complexity; and in the second its constant effort to impress upon its hearers the idea of a single, centralized India with a heroic tradition of her own as a formative and uniting impulse. It is in good sooth a monarch's dream of an imperial race. The Gupta Emperor of Pataliputra, who commissioned the last recension of this great epic, was as conscious as Ashoka before him or Akbar after; of making to his people the magic statement "India is one".
>
> India is a civilizational entity. Political unity has been a rare occurrence. Recorded history recalls only four such periods – the Imperial Mauryan era, the Gupta era, the Mughal era and the British rule. The Mahabharata's final recension was possibly committed to writing in its final form in the reign of Samudragupta (around AD 400) as an authoritative publication by an imperial central power. That is why all through Maharashtra, the Punjab and Bengal and South of the Vindhyas, Mahabharata is the same."

According to SB Roy, *Mahabharata*, as it is known today, consists in the main three layers. The original *Mahabharata*, known as 'Jaya' or the tale of battle and victory, was composed by Vyasa (Krishna Dwaipayan) himself. It must have been in the skeleton form. It was supposed to have only 8000 *shlokas*. The main text later on, which was recited by Rishi Viasampayana, was the second recension and it had approximately 24,000 *shlokas*. The third recension was the text recited by Rishi Ugrashrava Sauti which contained approximately 100,000 *shlokas*. It is of course quite possible that isolated intrapolations and even bulk intrapolations and alterations were made into this text. So *Mahabharata*, as it exists today, is perhaps a much larger work than what was originally composed.

Sister Nivedita asserts that in the Golden Age of India, the Imperial Guptas promulgated an 'official', authoritative version that spread the message of political unity – of India as not just a civilizational entity but as a political entity with an imperial past of splendour.

5

A Comparison : State of the Art— Sun Tzu and Mahabharata

Sun Tzu's *The Art of War* is regarded as a classic treatise on the art of war. It is an act of genius and the percepts contained in its thirteen chapters are still considered relevant in this day and age. It was written in a period of great military and intellectual ferment in China in the period of the warring kingdoms (450-300 BC). How does the Mahabharata compare as a military treatise with Sun Tzu's classic? Has it expounded any universal truisms and generalizations on war which could guide military thinking in our age?

The *Mahabharata* is a vast and rambling epic when contrasted with Sun Tzu's precise and specialist treatment. Yet the *Mahabharata's* military content is of profound interest. It is remarkable in one thing: it deals with combined arms operations. In fact it deals with the intricate and precise details of such combined arms formations, manoeuvres and battle drills. The armies described in the *Mahabharata* are 'Chaturangi' (four-armed or four-limbed). They comprise four basic arms – chariots, horsed cavalry, elephants and infantry. Sun Tzu's epic in contrast deals with infantry operations alone.

Just as a number of military schools had sprung up in China in the times of Sun Tzu, so also in the *Mahabharata*, we learn of various schools of war propounded by the learned Acharyas of that age. Some of the famous ones are Brihaspati, Shukracharya, Parashurama, Dronacharya, Kripacharya and Bhishma. These sages had propounded their own theories on the rules and practice of warfare. These military intellectuals offered their services/advice to the rulers of that age. Dronacharya, for instance, was appointed royal tutor to the princes of Hastinapur. Parashurama taught Bhishma, Karna and Dronacharya himself. Incidentally both Parashurama and Dronacharya were

Brahmins or intellectuals who made a living out of teaching the military arts.

The problem in comparison occurs basically due to the dispute about the historicity of the *Mahabharata*. Does it predate Sun Tzu's classic or is it a later development? Some Indologists put the age of the *Mahabharata* at 1400 BC, others as late as the eighth century AD. Sun Tzu belongs to the fourth century BC. We are however certain of the historical details of the contemporary Mauryan Army for these have been corroborated by the account of Megasthenes, the Greek Ambassador to Chandragupta Maurya's court (third century BC). The grand Mauryan Army comprised almost 650,000 men. It was divided into four arms and had an elephant corps of 9000, war chariots 8000, horsed cavalry 30,000 and infantry 600,000. This army was decidedly vastly superior and more sophisticated than the Chinese armies of Sun Tzu's period. It had developed bronze and iron weaponry and its military technology was far, far in advance of the Chinese. The Chinese Army had just one arm – the foot infantry. The Indian armies of the Mauryan period were highly sophisticated standing armies and had four arms.

It would therefore be historically more accurate to compare Kautilya's *Arthashastra* with Sun Tzu's classic. However, that should be the subject of a separate book by itself. On the issue of age and antiquity, the Indian tradition very definitely places the *Mahabharata* almost a thousand years before the Mauryan age. If that is indeed accurate, it represents a staggering advance over the Chinese in civilizational terms. Let us therefore carry out a detailed and comparative analysis of the military wisdom of the *Mahabharata* and Sun Tzu's classic *The Art of War*.

SUN TZU

Sun Tzu, the famous Chinese military theorist today, has a place in the sun. His writings have served to inspire no less a modern military thinker than Sir Basil Liddell Hart and the great Mao Zedong. Liddell Hart says that the 'seeds' of the 'Indirect Approach' were planted in his mind by Sun Tzu and TE Lawrence. The most quoted verse is from Chapter IV of Sun Tzu's classic, *The Art of War*, 'As water shapes its flow in accordance with the ground, so an army manages its victory in accordance with the situation of the enemy.' This (along with the deep penetration campaigns of the

Mongols under Ghengiz Khan) served as the basis of the 'Expanding Torrent' concept of armoured warfare which was used so devastatingly by the Germans in the Second World War, and the Israelis recently in 1956 and 1967.

Historical

25 years after the death of Confucius (429 BC) the leaders of Wei, Han and Chao states of China attacked the ruler of Chin and defeated him at Ching-Yang in 453 BC. With this began the *Period of the Warring States* (450-300 BC). There was incessant fighting between the six major states of China – Ch'i, Ch'u, Ch'in, Wei, Han and Chao. This turmoil lasted for 150 years. Bands of bandits infested the forested hills and reed-bordered lakes and terrorized the people. The political environment gave ample opportunity to self-styled military experts and scholars who wandered from one state to the other to peddle their ideas and theories to the kings and dukes. Sun Tzu was one of these theorists and *The Art of War* was composed in this period of intellectual ferment.

Development of Iron Technology in China

Iron was known in China by about 500 BC but it was only by 400 BC that many Chinese states had a flourishing iron industry to cater for arms and implements.

Reorganization of Armies

For the first time in China armies were reorganized from local levies system on to a sub-unit basis. Hereditary kings and feudal lords were replaced by professional officers and generals. The theory and practice of war were studied and the old chivalry gave place to an overwhelming emphasis on surprise and deception. Regular standing armies with a cohesive organization and excellent logistical back-up came into being. Recruitment was by conscription of peasants and the officers were professionals. The armies were led by specially selected shock troops. Elements of armies were capable of coordinated manoeuvre in accordance with detailed plans and were responsive to systematic signals by bells, gongs, drums and flags. The science of tactics was born.

Chi and Cheng Forces

This is a special characteristic of the Chinese military system.

(a) *Cheng Forces* were the regular orthodox armies (conventional armies) which were employed for the holding or fixing effort.
(b) *Chi Forces* were the special or elite elements used for speedy manoeuvre and shock actions to catch the enemy in the rear or deep flanks.

General Staff

The concept of a General Staff also emerged in this period. Staffs included numerous specialists like:

(a) Map makers and weather forecasters.
(b) Engineers for tunnelling and river crossing experts.

The science of logistics was developed, special attention was paid to morale, feeding of troops and a system of reward and punishment etc. Commanders who retreated without orders were beheaded.

State of the Art

Thus by the fourth century BC war in China had achieved a mature form, a form which indeed was not – *except for the employment of cavalry* – to be significantly altered for many hundreds of years. Thus though the Chinese possessed weapons of iron and were masters of offensive and defensive tactics, they were predominantly an *infantry or one arm army*. Sun Tzu is well-known for

(a) *His insistence upon surprise and deception*. Thus 'Make an uproar in the East, Strike in the West,' and 'The Thunder clap leaves no time to cover the Ears' (Chapter I.26) or 'All Warfare is based upon deception' (Chapter I, Verse 7) speak for themselves.
(b) *Use of the indirect approach*. 'As water has no constant form, there are in war no constant conditions.' (Chapter VI.29) The 'An Army is like water' (Chapter VI.28) analogy has already been quoted. 'Speed is the Essence of War.' (Chapter XI.29) 'Go into emptiness, strike voids, bypass what he defends, hit him where he does not expect you.'

(c) *Concept of supreme excellence.* 'To capture the enemy army is better than to destroy it.' (Chapter III.2) 'For to win one hundred victories in one hundred battles is not the acme of skill. To *subdue the enemy without fighting is the acme of skill* and supreme excellence.' (Chapter III.3) 'The *supreme excellence in war is to attack the enemy's plans.*'

(d) *Target mind of enemy commander.* 'Anger his general, confuse him.' (Chapter I.22). *'The responsibility for a martial host of a million lies in one man. He is the trigger of its spirit.'* (Chapter III.30) 'To a surrounded enemy you must leave a way of escape – show him there is a road to safety and to create an idea in his mind that there is an alternative to death. Then strike.' (Chapter VI.31)

These are some of the highlights of the 13 Chapters of *The Art of War*. The Chinese military idiom appears more graphic and telling but it must be borne in mind that *The Art of War* was more or less a professional training manual whereas the *Mahabharata* was a wide-ranging epic of encyclopaedic proportions.

COMPARISON – STATE OF ART

(a) *Antiquity*. The *Mahabharata* at 1400 BC predates Sun Tzu by about one thousand years.

(b) *Weapons technology.* Iron was reportedly used a thousand years in advance of China.

(c) *All-arms team concept*. There were four basic arms in the Mahabharata armies. The chariots, the elephants, the cavalry and the infantry. Sun Tzu's *magnum opus* seems to deal only with infantry operations.

(d) *Insistence on the indirect approach*. Has a lot in common with *Kuta Yudha* methodology as propagated by Krishna, Ashwathama, Brihaspati and Shukracharya in India.

(e) *Target – Mind of enemy commander*. There is a common insistence in both cases on this aspect.

(f) *Battle drills* are specifically mentioned as *vyuhas in the Mahabharata* and deal with combined arms operations. Cavalry came much later in China.

(g) *Espionage system*. Seems equally developed in both eras but the *Mahabharata* provides far more elaborate details of intelligence organizations and operations.

(h) *Insistence on surprise and deception*. The Chinese emphasis is much greater but it is not totally absent in the Indian epic. Once again Krishna and Brihaspati and Ashwathama can be cited.

(j) *Administration and man management* is equally stressed in both epics but greater details are available in the *Mahabharata*.

(k) *War as a last resort*. This theme is more prevalent in the Indian school which advocates graduated or flexible responses – to covert diplomacy and covert operations. Sun Tzu also does not condone butchery for the sake of killing but advocates superior strategy to subdue the enemy without fighting.

BALANCE

In the overall balance both schools of war appear equally matched but for two glaring facts to the contrary:

(a) The Indian school deals with combined arms operations while the Chinese school deals with a single arm alone.

(b) The Indian school at 1400 BC seems to *predate the Chinese by a thousand years*. However, this conclusion is subject to the validation of the actual age of the *Mahabharata*. A much more accurate historical comparison is between the Mauryan armies of Chandragupta and the Chinese armies of the Sun Tzu period. The Indian forces and state of the art are decidedly superior.

(c) The obvious superiority of Sun Tzu however lies in his explicit emphasis on surprise and deception as opposed to the 'direct' and frontal approach of the Indians. Krishna and a number of contemporary Indian 'Acharyas' however also tried to emphasize this aspect. The fact however is little known precisely because the influence of this school has been rather limited. The Mahabharata seems to be premised doctrinally on a Paradigm based on "Attrition" as opposed to "manoeuvre". It places heavy reliance on force on force, head on engagements in which one side wears the other down by sheer attrition. It is premised upon an anahilation and destruction of the enemy in a set piece battle usually in a flat, wide open battle area or plain which permits the coordinated applications of four distinct manoeuvre masses— the chariots, the elephants, the cavalry and the infantry.

6

Sources of Indian Military Thought

The fountainhead of the Indian thought on war can be traced back to the Vedic times. The Vedas contain innumerable references to war and the exploits of famous kings and warriors. But the Vedas are not a treatise on war. Just as in China, many ancient schools of war existed in India in ancient times.

The following could be deemed to be the source of classical Indian military thought. They are listed in an approximate chronological order:

(a) *The Dhanurveda*. One of the *Upa-Vedas*, along with *Ayurveda* (Medicine), *Gandharva Veda* (Dance and Music) and *Sthapatya Veda* (Architecture), it deals with the art of archery.

(b) *Manu Smriti*. The code of the Hindu law giver Manu.

(c) *Shukra Neeti*. The military aphorisms of the sage Shukracharya said to be the military theorist of the *asuras*.

(d) *The Mahabharata*. Especially *Bhishma Parva* and *Shanti Parvas*. Military wisdom is spread throughout this epic. It provides a vast overview of the contending schools of military thought in that period. Not only does it serve as a source of military theory, but being an epic, it is equally a historical record of an actual war.

(e) Kautilya's *Arthashastra* (300 BC). Written by the famous Machiavelli of India, Chanakya. It is a unique military classic by any standards and its advocacy of ruthless statecraft would serve as an object lesson even for present-day exponents of the art. It is surprising that this excellent and matchless repository of military wisdom finds no Indian students today. It is the right book for comparison with Sun Tzu's classic and merits separate study by itself.

(f) *The Puranas*. As per PE Pargiter, they represent the Kshatriya tradition of history and legend preserved by the bards and completely independent of the Brahminical tradition. The *Puranas* contain a wealth of information on the art and science of war. There are 18 *Mahapuranas* (Main) and 18 *Upa-Puranas* (Sub). Some of the useful *Puranas* from the military theory aspect are:

- Agni Purana
- Matsya Purana
- Bradharma Purana

In this study we shall confine ourselves primarily to the *Mahabharata* period of military thought and evolution.

Schools of War in Ancient India

From these sources it appears that around the period of the *Mahabharata* (1400 BC), there were five schools of war in ancient India. They can be listed under two broad heads based upon the direct and the indirect approaches.

Direct approach (Dharma Yudha)	*Indirect approach* (Kuta Yudha)
Sadashiva Dhanurveda Concept of War	Brihaspati's School of War
Bhishma's School of War	Krishna's School of War
	Shukracharya's School of War
	Ashwathama's School of War

DIRECT APPROACH
(Dharma/Nyaya Yudha)

Bhishma's School of War

Bhishma, the grandsire of the Kauravas and the Pandavas is the grand old man of the *Mahabharata*. He stands out as a man of impeccable integrity and character. In valour and military skill he stands unsurpassed and unrivalled. In fact he was called 'Bhishma's (the terrible one) because of the very exacting oath of celibacy that he had taken. In keeping with his character, the school of war propounded by Bhishma is marked by chivalry and humanism. There is a conscious attempt to inject decency into the murder and mayhem of war.

Nyaya/Dharma Yudha (Ethical or Just War)

Bhishma propounded this concept of a Just War. This was something in common with Roman law which also made a distinction between 'Just' and 'Unjust' war (based upon an analysis of its causes or motives). This principle was later developed and extended by Christian theologians (especially St Thomas Aquinas). However they tended to take a very subjective view of what was 'Just' and 'Unjust'. Subsequently, all actions by the enemy were classed as 'Unjust' while all measures taken by own forces were 'Just'.

However, *Dharma Yudha* in Bhishma's dispensation meant that not only the motives or cause of the war had to be 'just' and 'ethical' but even its *conduct*. *Dharma Yudha*, according to him, was the honest trial of strength and military skill. Wars were to be fought with strict adherence to codes of military ethics and chivalry. All surprise and deception were totally taboo and unchivalrous. Under the influence of Bhishma and Yudhisthira the Mahabharata was largely fought on these ethical principles. The very fact that today ethical conduct in war is governed by the Geneva Convention shows that such an ethical or moral overtone is not totally out of context even in modern warfare. What should interest the student of military thought, however, is the fact that these ethical codes of chivalry were often violated by both sides. The Pandavas under the guidance of Krishna often resorted to *Kuta Yudha* – the indirect approach based on surprise, deception and subterfuge. *That is how they won the war.*

As would be obvious to any student of Indian military history, the influence of the traditions of *Dhanurveda* and Bhishma is still very active at a collective subconscious level. This tendency to stick to a chivalrous mode of war, relying only upon valour for victory has persisted throughout Indian military history, and is one of its chief failings. The insistence upon the direct approach has been very costly for us. In fact Shivaji stands out as the only proponent of the other Indian school of war – based upon the indirect approach, *Kuta Yudha*. The tragedy is that just because it has so few followers we have elected to forget the fact that it existed.

However, the Bhishma school of war needs to be studied because of the great influence it still subconsciously exerts on the Indian military mind.

These can best be gleaned from Bhishma's aphorisms on the ethics of war and on the principles of war that he enunciated.

Ethics of war (as expounded by Bhishma to Yudhisthira in *Shanti Parva*)

A few of them were :

(a) *Dharma*. A king should always take the side of *Dharma*, i.e. truth and justice. If he cannot decide where *Dharma* lies he should abstain from war.

(b) If the opponent is honest and religious attempts should be made for a *diplomatic solution*. War must be the last recourse.

(c) *A king must not attack or kill the following :*

- A man not in armour.
- A man with his weapons broken or carrier mount/vehicle destroyed.
- Wounded persons.
- One stunned or benumbed by the shock of wounds or battle.
- One fleeing from the battlefield.

(d) *Poison arrows must not be used*. One cannot help noticing the striking similarity between these injunctions and the modern Geneva Conventions. In addition to this standard code to limit attrition rates during the course of the Mahabharata War Bhishma at one stage suggested a policy of :

(e) *Graduated response/flexible response*. If one side starts a war of words, he said, the other should limit its response to the verbal level and so on.

(f) *Battles must be fought between equals*. Chariots must attack chariots, cavalry must fight cavalry and so on. Warning must precede such offensives.

(g) *Non-combatants and administrative personnel* must not be attacked.

(h) All combat must be restricted to the daylight hours alone.

The Concept of Honour

This has come down to us from the Sada Shiva *Dhanurveda* and Bhishma and still enthuses modern Indian soldiers. It says that death in battle is a very noble and honourable death indeed. For a soldier death by weapons was a thousand times superior to death by illness or old age.

Principles of War

Bhishma's principles of war are spread all over the *Mahabharata*. A few notable ones are:

(a) *Campaign season*. The months of Agrahayana (November-December) to Chaitra (March-April) are the ideal campaigning seasons in the subcontinent. (How true it is till today!) This time stipulation, so Bhishma said, should be violated only if victory otherwise is certain or the enemy is in deep trouble.

(b) *Methods of war must be varied* to combat the nature and genius of the adversary, i.e. an honest and chivalrous enemy must be fought by honourable methods, but a cunning and deceitful enemy must be dealt with in a similar manner.

(c) *Influence of climate on employment of arms*:

- *Dry season*. Use chariots and cavalry.
- *Rainy season*. Use elephants and infantry.

(d) *Influence of terrain on employment of arms* :

- *Flat and open country*. Use chariots and cavalry.
- *Ground with dwarf trees and thinly built-up areas*. Use elephants.
- *Hill, forests and areas dominated by forts*. Use infantry.

(e) *Approach marches* must be over main arteries and roads the security of which has been assessed by own spies and informers. This keeps the troops fresh.

(f) *Concentration areas* for infantry however can be in forests which afford good concealment. A level area near a forest is the best battleground.

(g) *Ethnic considerations*. Before employing a particular army study the racial characteristics and military traditions of its troops carefully. Employ them in accordance with their innate genius and capabilities. Thus Bhishma discusses the following Indian troops:

- *Soldiers of Gandhara, Sindhu and Saubir* are well-built, tall and courageous. Experts in 'Nakhra' and 'Prasa'.
- *Eastern troops* are clever and quick on the uptake. They are diplomatic in nature and are experts at fighting from elephants.
- *Yavanas (Greeks) and troops from Kambara and Mathura* are individualistic and experts in duels.

(h) *Man management and motivation. 'The world can be conquered with a handful of soldiers if they are contented*! (This appears to be a paraphrase of *Shlokas* 212 and 213 of the *Sadashiva Dhanurveda* which states that 500 loyal soldiers can defeat a vast army).

(j) *Freedom of manoeuvre*. This should not be lost by taking shelter in a fort and resorting to static warfare.

(k) *Scorched earth*. However if attacked by a very powerful enemy the king may withdraw to a fort which has been very well stocked after destroying all food and provisions that are outside so as to deny them to the enemy. Defence is a last resort.

THE INDIRECT APPROACH (Kuta Yudha)

As mentioned earlier under the head of the indirect approach we had the following schools of thought in the *Mahabharata* period:

(a) Brihaspati's School of War.
(b) Krishna's School of War.
(c) Shukracharya's School.
(d) Ashwathama's School.

Brihaspati's School of War

Brihaspati, the legendary preceptor of the 'Gods' (Aryans?), is a military theorist who is liberally quoted by various kings in the *Mahabharata*. His school (as gleaned from his various sayings) appears pragmatic and ruthless and much more in consonance with modern military practice. There are some curious similarities with the works of Sun Tzu. Some of his principles, as mentioned at various places in the *Mahabharata* are:

(a) *Attack superiority ratio*. Attack the enemy only if his strength is one-third of your own (*Udyog Parva*). It is interesting to note that our own insistence on 3:1 superiority for attack today has 2500 years of historical sanction!

(b) *Avoid war if the enemy is strong*. Try and appease him with good behaviour or giving gifts of money – but preserve the will to kill him when the opportune moment comes. In the meantime try and weaken him by:

- Diplomatic manoeuvre.
- Use of agents and saboteurs (*Shanti Parva*).

(c) If the enemy strength equals your own seek truce through *treaties* and avoid confrontation (*Salya Parva*).

(d) *Consolidate your forces* if inferior in number to the enemy – expand them if superior.

(e) If war with a numerically stronger enemy is forced on you concentrate your troops by adopting the *'Needle Head' formation* (Suchi-Mukha Vyuha) (*Bhishma Parva*).

(f) *Never trust the enemy or spare him*. Opportunity once wasted never returns (*Shanti Parva*).

(g) *Spare no one* however old or virtuous if he comes as the enemy.

The Krishna School of War

To Krishna goes the unique distinction of being not only a powerful warrior and field commander, but also of being an equally effective statesman and diplomat. The Germans, as we all know, had separated the staff and command functions into specialist categories but in following the British system of alternating staff with command appointments we seem to have fallen back upon the ancient Indian practice as exemplified by Krishna. The victory of the Pandavas can be ascribed to the advice of Krishna for adopting *Kuta Yudha* methodology (the indirect approach) at every crucial juncture of the Kurukshetra War. The fact that even at that time such methods were strongly resisted highlights the central failing of Indian military thought – its penchant for the direct approach characterized by a lot of bravado and pointless chivalry – even at the cost of victory.

The end justifies the means

That is the keynote of Krishna's military philosophy. He has laid great stress on:

(a) *Deception*. In war the truth may often have to be sacrificed in pursuit of victory (*Karna Parva*).

(b) *Subterfuge*. Bluffing is as virtuous as truthfulness to gain victory in war (*Karna Parva*).

(c) *Relentless offensive action*. Never allow respite to a weakened enemy. Even a good man would acquire fame by exploiting the troubles of an enemy to defeat him. Krishna thereby stressed the annihilation of he enemy by unremitting offensive actions (*Karna Parva*).

(d) *Use cunning methods* to defeat an enemy if he is superior in strength or capability (*Salya Parva*).

Subsequently, in this book, the greatness of Krishna as a general and strategist of the indirect approach will be highlighted by relevant examples from the Mahabharata battle.

Shukracharya's School of War

Shukracharya is said to be the military theorist (*acharya*) of the *daityas* or *asuras* (Dravidians?). He, like Brihaspati and Krishna, stresses the indirect approach by advocating deception measures to achieve surprise. He also advocates annihilation of the enemy without any moral scruples. His quotations appear predominantly in the *Salya Parva* of the *Mahabharata*.

Ashwathama's School of War

Ashwathama was the son of the famous military teacher of the Kauravas and Pandavas, Dronacharya. His articulation of the indirect approach almost appears savage in its vehemence. In the *Sauptik Parva* he says, '*In war there is nothing unjust or unvirtuous. It is best to attack the enemy when he is tired, sleeping, leaderless, scattered or wavering, or having his meals or has entered refuge.*' In pursuance of this it must be mentioned that Ashwathama put into practice what he preached. He is the only warrior who flouted the code of not fighting at night and at the termination of the Mahabharata War launched a murderous raid on the Pandava camp and inflicted terrible casualties. This was then a flagrant violation of the ground rules of war agreed upon by both sides.

These schools of war have been further crystallized by Kautilya in his epic, *Arthashastra*, which in effect represents the quintessence of the military wisdom of the epic period as refined and transmitted down the centuries. The *Puranas* have also carried forth these traditions. However Kautilya's *Arthashastra* reflects the response of the Indian civilisation to the challenge of the Greek invasion. Here the indirect approach to war comes strongly to the fore. Kautilya laid great emphasis on covert actions and destabilisation operations as also psychological war and information operations to weaken and unbalance an enemy before launching a conventional military attack. This will be analysed in detail in subsequent chapter.

CHIVALRY
THE DIRECT VS THE INDIRECT APPROACH

While discussing the various schools of war in ancient India we had described the school of chivalry and righteous conduct in war as prescribed by Bhishma and the more ruthless schools of Krishna, Brihaspati, Shukracharya and others who allowed no place for any charitable sentiment towards the enemy. However, this innate chivalry appears to be deeply rooted in the Indian psyche and has always resisted the employment of the indirect approach in many subsequent wars. In the *Mahabharata*, fortunately, the views of Krishna, the grand strategist of the Pandavas, prevailed, and by recourse to deception, subterfuge and psychological warfare aimed at the minds of the enemy commanders, the Pandavas won an overwhelming victory. There lies a great lesson for us.

Prakshya and Aprakshya Yudha

This is another interesting concept of the epic period which is analogous to modern overt and covert war.

(a) *Prakshya Yudha* implied *overt and a declared war* or state of hostilities – same as *Nyaya Yudha*.

(b) *Aprakshya Yudha* implied that no war was declared overtly but continuous *covert operations* undertaken by agents and suboteurs to spread discord and disaffection, to assassinate important persons and to poison wells and destroy crops. This was part of the *Kuta Yudha* methodology and speaks volumes of the high level of statecraft in those days. The similarities with recent theories expounded by scholars of our Institute of Defence Studies and Analyses of the use of force without war with this concept are quite remarkable.

Krishna as a Strategist

As is obvious from the study of Krishna's principles of war, he was a ruthless strategist who had grasped the essentials of the indirect approach in those early days. He himself was a great warrior and his feats of physical prowess have been embellished in legend, song and dance. It is said that both the Pandavas and Kauravas requested him simultaneously to fight on their behalf. Keeping a neutral stand he offered his armies to one and his services in an advisory capacity to the other. The Kauravas opted for the 'brawn' element, the army, while the Pandavas gratefully accepted him as their Chief of Staff. So Krishna became the charioteer of Arjuna, the best car warrior and archer amongst the Pandavas (the Commander-in-Chief of the Pandava army). As it turned out the Pandava choice of 'brains' proved far superior to the 'brawn' element taken by Duryodhana. Thus, though numerically far superior (11:7) the 'exchange rate' tilted in favour of the Pandavas due to superior strategy and generalship and the overall unity in the higher direction of war as opposed to the discord and personality clashes that characterized the Kauravas' higher command set-up. Krishna was specifically responsible for:

(a) *Rallying the spirits of Arjuna* who had lost the will to fight before the commencement of the battle. This psychological conditioning is enshrined in the famous Hindu scripture of the *Gita* – which provides a coherent philosophy of fighting to all men in arms. It has a message which is universal, that goes beyond the uniform to all men of action – all over the world. It teaches all soldiers how to manage the terms disorganising emotions of "fear" and "guilt" in war.

(b) *The killing of Bhishma*. This was made possible when the Pandavas accepted Krishna's advice, put down their arms and went and requested Bhishma for advice on how to kill him. It is a measure of the superb moral fibre and kindness of the man that he told them how to do it. They exploited his ethical disposition to bring about his end. They employed the same method the next day and eliminated Bhishma.

(c) *The killing of Jayadratha*. Jayadratha had treacherously killed Abhimanyu, the son of Arjuna, in the famous *chakravyuha* episode. Arjuna had sworn to kill him by dusk the next day or commit suicide. The Kauravas accordingly made a superb defensive array around the prime target, Jayadratha, and prevented Arjuna from killing him. Nightfall came and the Kauravas rejoiced. Jayadratha came out triumphantly from his secure position. Krishna exhorted Arjuna to ignore all chivalry and kill him instantly. This he did and redeemed his pledge.

(d) *The death of Dronacharya*. The elimination of Dronacharya, the great military teacher of the epic period, was also caused by the advice of Krishna. In all Krishna therefore was responsible for the elimination of all key commanders of the opposite camp. He also ensured that the will to fight of his own key commanders never flagged in the conduct of this 'short-duration but very high-intensity' conflict. He was a past master of the art of psychological warfare. He can rightly be called the prime architect of the Pandava victory.

Psychological Warfare – The War of the Mind

All through the course of this war the Pandavas, under the advice of Krishna, resorted to Psy Wars to weaken the enemy's will to fight, to play adversely upon the minds of key commanders, and even to spread discord in the enemy camp. Following are some examples:

(a) *Propaganda measures*. These were directed to win over the hearts and minds of enemy troops and soften attitudes of key commanders. Thus Yudhisthira before the commencement of hostilities left his weapons to pay respects to the senior commanders of the opposite side – notably the veterans like Bhishma and Dronacharya.

(b) *Subversion*. While in the midst of the Kaurava armies Yudhisthira announced that he was waging a war of *Dharma* (justice and righteousness). Any man who still wished to come over to his side was welcome. It is said that Prince Yuyussu actually defected at this stage along with his troops to the Pandava army.

(c) *Disinformation*. The only psychological chink in Dronacharya's mental make-up was his extreme attachment to his son Ashwathama. Krishna advised Bhima to kill an elephant named Ashwathama and announce that Ashwathama was dead. This news was ratified by Yudhisthira, who had a reputation for honesty. This news so completely shattered the redoubtable Dronacharya that he totally lost his will to fight. In that state of psychological collapse he was easily killed.

(d) *Concerted psychological campaign to nullify key personnel*. Salya was the charioteer of Karna. Yudhisthira prevailed upon him to constantly irritate Karna by exaggerating the powers of Arjuna, his hated rival. He did not manoeuvre Karna's chariot properly and constantly fought with him and abused him. This so harassed and exasperated the irritable Karna that he was in a considerable state of confusion when the crucial moment of the battle came. The invincible Karna was thus defeated by exploiting the chinks in his psychological make-up.

(e) *The use of war drums, conches and bugles*. This is very widespread in the Mahabharata War. These were used both for signalling as well as frightening the enemy and raising the morale of own troops.

Information Warfare

The world is today in the throes of a Revolution in Military Affairs that seeks to effect a synthesis of Information technology, Electronic warfare and Psychological warfare with the force multipliers of the mass media (like television) to give rise to a radical new form of war that seeks to attack the mind of the adversary. This collective mind has today acquired a largely informational and electronic character. Hence the modern concept of attacking the Information and Electronic architecture (the info-structure) and disabling the critical information nodes. The attack on the mind was well known to the ancients. A verse in the Atharva Veda says, "Speak to our enemies O wardrum, we bring upon our adversaries hatred, panic, discord and confusion of mind." A number of mythical incantations in the Atharva Veda and later in the Tantric literature were supposedly used to attack the mind of the enemy. The veracity and efficacy of such mystical incantations to induce psychological mal-effects may be doubtful and debatable. However, the Mahabharata, and later the Arthashastra, dwell in great detail upon highly sophisticated psychological warfare and Information/Deception operations. Krishna, the grand strategist of the Kurukshetra War, had drawn up a detailed psychological profile of all the key enemy commanders. Their psychological vulnerabilities were brilliantly analysed and attacked. Drona was obsessively attached to his son Ashwathama. Deliberate disinformation about his death caused the redoubtable Dronacharya to become a psychologcal wreck. He lost the will to fight and slumped down in his chariot. He was easily killed in this state. Karna was a great warrior. His psychological chink was his quick temper and irritability. Shalya, his charioteer, was exploited to irritate him constantly and put him in a haze of confusion in which he made fatal mistakes. The chivalrous Bhishma would not attack a eunuch. Shikhandi, the eunuch was made to lead the attack against him. The examples are endless and do point out to very clear insights into the psychological dimensions of war. Spies and agents were used to spread rumors and disinformation and create dissension in enemy ranks. Though some of the examples cited seem simplistic or even naive by the present day standards of sophistication, they nevertheless indicate a very clear grasp of the psychological and informational aspects of war and the need to attack and paralyze the mind of the enemy commander.

7

Fighting Arms of the Ancient Indian Armies : A Historic Evaluation

"Where there are Elephants there is Victory"

The basic Indian concept of Chaturangi or "Four limbed" Armies merits a more detailed discussion and historical analysis. It is a primal civilisational motif and represents the flowering of the Indian military genius into a war form that was peculiarly Indian. This organisational form of war stabilised around the fourth century BC and remained more or less constant till the Muslim Invasion in the 10th and 11th centuries AD.

Historic Evaluation. The Infantry foot soldier or Paditi was the primal warrior of the Indian civilisation. As the civilisational spaces for its expression expanded to encompass the entire subcontinent and its peripheral regions (including Afghanistan) it became apparent that the Foot soldier had to give way to better means of military mobility. Unfortunately, the Subcontinent lacked a good gene pool of horses. Even though these were extensively employed in war, the Indian horsed Cavalry never reached the technical sophistication of the Greek, Mongol, Arab, or Mughal Cavalry. The bits were archaic and saddles and stirrups were largely unknown. The bulk of the Indian horsed Cavalry soldiers either rode bare back or on blankets. Unlike as in the Greek and Mongol Armies, horsed archers were unknown in India. It was the superiority of the Central Asian and Arab Cavalry that was to cost the Indian civilisation dearly from the 10th century onwards. The Horse in India was primarily a means of mobility and did not evolve into a true fighting platform. It would therefore be useful to chronologically trace the evolution of the various Arms in India and their impact on our military fortunes.

Vedic Armies. P.C. Chakravarti in his magnum opus (The Art of War in Ancient India) highlights that Armies in the Vedic period had two basic arms - the foot soldier (patti) and the car-warriors (Rathis) or Chariot Corps. The Vedic Chariots were light platforms of two wheels and pulled by two horses. The wheels were initially wooden wheels but later gave way to lighter and more sophisticated spoked wheels. The crew consisted of two, the charioteer or driver and the car warrior or the Jedi Knight. The Vedic battle chariot was a great war innovation of its time. It could carry the battle crew long distances without fatigue. They were fresh for battle at the end of their approach marches. They were able to carry a large amount of ordnance (in the form of arrows, spears or javelins) and the chariot structure itself provided protection to its crew. Towards the end of the Vedic period, we see the gradual transformation of this two limbed Army organisation into a classical four arms or Chaturangi organisational format. Chakravarti feels that by the time of the Jatakas - this "Chaturangi-bala" or "Chaturanga-camu" - military organisation had standardised in India. The four basic arms were the Infantry (Pati or Paditi), the Cavalry (Ashwa), the Chariots (Ratha) and the Elephant Corps (or Gaja). One would beg to differ. This four fold Army organisational form is clearly mentioned in the Mahabharata as a very well established war form that had reached a post-Vedic stage of maturation. The Mahabharata infact was a civilisational Armageddon in which this matured war form found its fullest expression in the form of Chaturangi or four armed armies. The prime combat arm in the Mahabharata period was the Chariot Corps. We now hear of chariots that are two or four wheeled and drawn by two, three four or even eight horses. These war chariots were the pride of the Indian Armies of those days. The great Archers who fought in them were the famed Jedi knights of their era. They were the central characters of that Homeric war even as Ajax, Achillies and Hector are the great Greek heroes of the Illiad. The military history of that period is largely the hagiographic and laudatory accounts of the exploits of these car warriors or "heroes" or Jedi knights. War, then still had a simplistic format. It was the direct test of combat power in a designated battle area that lent itself to the operation of the four arms of both the opposing armies. The grand plain of Kurukshetra was such a historic battle field. The war chariots found their full tactical expression in this terrain. The car warriors were the Jedi knights of that era and are said to have inflicted horrendous slaughter on the ancient battle field. The historical fact is that the Mahabharata War left the basic imprimatur of military organisation in India that was basically to remain unchanged till the 10th century A.D. All that actually changed was the degree of emphasis on the individual Arms.

The Transition from Chariots to Elephants. The first historic military invasion of India was the military expedition launched by Alexander. The Greek Infantry phalanxes and Horsed Cavalry had been honed into excellent instruments of military mobility through a series of internecine wars fought between the Greek city states. These conflicts helped Alexander to train and hone the Greek Armies into an excellent military instrument of conquest. The exploits of Alexander and his Greek phalanxes and Cavalry were a historic break-through in the art of war. The wars between the Greek City states served as a combat laboratory where the tactics and battle drills were honed to perfection. The Greek Armies subsequently set new standards of mobility and reach that transformed the nature of war itself. From Greece they broke into Asia and defeated the mighty Persian Empire. Alexander ranged into the lush valleys of Ferghana in the Central Asian oasis and entered Afghanistan - then the outposts of the Indian civilisational landscape. There was then no central political authority in North-Western India. The Nanda Empire was focussed in the East— largely in the lower flood plains of the Indo-Gangetic system. The North-western quadrant of India was a confused mosaic of petty principalities and minor kingdoms. There was no central Indian power to contest the Greek military invasion of the North-West. Reputedly, Chanakya (the redoubtable Kautilya) appealed to the Mahapadma Nanda, the Emperor to discharge his civilisational duty and contest the Greek advance. The Nanda king apparently was in a drunken stupor when Chanakya came to his court. Legend has it that he insulted Chankya and had him rudely thrown out. The enraged Chankya decided there and then that the Nanda king had become unfit to rule. Indian civilisational unity had now to be transformed into actual political unity if it was to be saved from the depredations of foreign invaders. The rest of the Chanakya's life was spent in trying to bring about the political and military unification of the Ancient Indian civilisation. In response to the Greek Military challenge to the Indian civilisation, Chanakya and his young disciple

Chandragupta went to India's North West to cobble up unity in the face of the foreign invader. To his dismay, he found that internecine feuds had opened the way for the invader. Ambhi, the ruler of Taxshila (now in Afghanistan) had been humiliated in battle by Porous - the chieftain of the Trans Jhelum tracts. Ambhi had joined up with Alexander. It was left to Porus to meet the Greek invasion head on. Porus reportedly had an army of 30,000 Infantry, 4000 Cavalry, 300 Chariots and 200 war elephants. In the Mahabharatan tradition this four armed Army was primed for combat in a designated battlefield. It was still premised on the Attrition paradigm of the Mahabharatan War tradition. It was not geared for the more mobile operations of the class that Alexander had introduced. The two armies were ranged across the River Hydaspes (Jhelum). Alexander's agile horsed Cavalry had the edge in mobility. It effected a river crossing downstream after many ruses. When the Chariots of Porus were rushed to block this river crossing they simply bogged down in the muddy river banks. The Chariots lacked cross country mobility and were good only for the flat and hard surface of designated battle plains. Alexander had enunciated a new Paradigm of war. The biggest shock to Alexander's Greek Armies however were the 200 war elephants of Porus. Alexander won the battle. His troops however were truly shaken by their first encounter with the War Elephants. These were monstrous and terrifying beasts. The psychological shock effect of these on the Greek troops was considerable. The redoubtable Chanakya was dismayed by this first Indian defeat at the hands of an alien civilisation. The Nanda Empire was not willing to discharge its civilisational duty. As per the Greek historian, Agrammes king of Gangaride and the Parisi reportedly had an Army of 200,000 Infantry, 80,000 Cavalry, 300 Chariots and 6000 war Elephants. He was however not willing to commit them to combat in a forward mode. He would rather wait for this civilisational menace to reach him first before he responded to it. He was not interested in a forward defence well ahead of his realm. He was simply not prepared to think in terms of an Indian civilisational entity beyond his Nanda Kingdom of Magadha. Kautilya had moved up and closely studied the Greek military methodology. He realised the technical limitations of the chariot for a more mobile form of war. He fully realised the psychological shock effect of the war elephants on the Greek Armies. The war elephant he recokened had matching and even superior mobility to the Greek Cavalry. *It was this that led Kautilya to down grade the importance of war chariots and raise the war elephants to the pride of place in the Indian military system.* It was to become the prime shock Arm later of the Imperial Mauryan military machine.

Psy War Campaign. Dismayed by the Nanda's abdication of their civilisational duty, Chanakya now launched a very skillful psy war campaign that halted the Greek Army in its tracks. The Greek military machine was at the end of its reach. It had over stretched itself. It had been fighting non stop now for years. It had come far from home into strange and unknown lands. The sight of the terrifying war beasts had shaken them to the core. Skillfully, Kautilya analysed the Greek state of morale and devised very brilliant psy warfare themes that would exploit the shock of this new weapon system. He now sent his spies and saboteurs to the Greek military camps. They spread rumors of the strength of the Nanda Army. Porus was just a border chieftain. He had a mere 200 war elephants. The Nanda military machine had over 6000 war elephants. The spies greatly magnified the actual number of war elephants and the size and efficiency of the Nanda Army.

World's First Information Operation

The tired and battle weary Greeks heard these livid tales around their camp fires. The Indian courtesans they slept with spread vivid themes of gigantic and monstrous hordes of war elephants that would trample their armies. The merchants and wandering mendicants confirmed these rumors. They talked of how the Elephants were used to crush the skulls of their victims and trample humans under foot. The rumors multiplied and spread like wild fire amongst the Greek ranks. The result of one of the world's most sophisticated psy war campaigns was electrifying. The Greek Army became restive. Then the unthinkable happened. The Greeks mutinied. They had had enough. They were home sick and they wanted to go back home while they could. The unknown dread of facing thousands of monstrous beasts was terrifying. Skillfully the world's first master of Information war had woven his themes and achieved the miracle. He stopped a victorious world conquering Army cold in its tracks. He did so without firing a shot or an arrow. He simply caused the Greek Army to mutiny. The Greek Army forced Alexander to turn back. All his fiery oratory was of no use in the face of this brilliant Information operation. The Greeks would have none of his promises of glory and riches. The saddened Alexander gave up. He was too good a military commander to ignore the psychological state of his tired Army. He realised the one challenge that would now rouse it again to great military effort - the challenge of getting back home with the booty. The celebrated Greek invasion of India thus became in effect an extended border raid. Alexander now advanced down the Indus flood plain to get to the sea and head for home. Thus the Greek invasion of India ended on a somewhat tame and muted note.

The Consolidation

Having turned the Greek Armies back with a brilliantly successful Information warfare campaign, Kautilya now turned his energies to transforming the Indian civilisational entity into a political entity that would be conscious of defending its territorial and cultural integrity. In another series of successful information operations he arrayed an alliance of Indian kingdoms against the Nandas and overthrew this decadent regime. He then installed Chandragupta on the throne and set the stage for the primal political unification of India under the Imperial Mauryan Banner. India's bane was its splintering into a host of petty kingdoms and fiefdoms that undid the civilisational unity. To safeguard the Indic civilisation it was essential to transform its civilisational unity into a political consolidation and this was the prime contribution of the legendary Kautilya. In a short time the Mauryan empire militarily consolidated the whole of the sub-continent. Not content with this, Chanakya exhorted Chandragupta to secure Afghanistan by throwing out the last remenants of Greek power from the invasion route. As per Professor Chakravarti, *he now transformed the Mauryan military machine so that the prime arm status now shifted from Chariots to the Shock Arm - The Elephant Corps. An adage of that period said, "Where there are elephants there is victory."* Kautilya himself wrote "It is on elephants that the destruction of an enemy's Army depends" and again "The victory of kings in battles depends mainly on elephants." Palakapya, the author of the Hastayur Veda said, "The elephant is the ornament of the Army." The Elephant was eminently suited for mobile warfare in all kinds of terrain. With this rebuilt war machine, centered around a corps of some 9000 war elephants (and 8000 chariots, 30,000 Cavalry and 650,000 Infantry), the imperial Mauryan Army now attacked the Greek Satrap Selukas Niketor and threw his Armies out of Afghanistan and Baluchistan. Selukas ceded the three Satrapies of Asia

(Heart), Arachosia (Kandhar) and Paropanasadoi (Kabul). He gave his daughter in marriage to Chandragupta and received in exchange a gift of 500 war elephants. *Chandragupta Maurya had achieved what his British successors would sigh for in vain some 2000 years later - a scientific frontier for India that secured the invasion routes via Afghanistan.*

The Elephant thus became the prime shock arm of the Indian Armies. Its employment had considerable shock value. It put the Indian war leader on a high mount where his entire Army could see him. This was critical for the Armies of that period which cohered round the charismatic personality of their emperor or King. Subsequently this also proved to be the undoing of the Elephant as a war mount. When explosives, gun powder and artillery entered the fray, the Elephant became highly unreliable. The terrified giant could not be controlled and was indiscriminate in his flight. In the battle between Mohammad Ghazni and Prithiviraj, the elephants on which the Indian princes rode became unruly when the Afghans fired burning naptha arrows on them. They fled and thus the Rajput armies were demoralised by the uncontrolled exit of their princes and commanders from the battlefield. Mohamad Bin Kasim used similar tactics when he invaded Dahir's kingdom in Sindh. Dahir was seated on the howdah atop his prize war elephant. Kasim asked his naptha throwers to target him. They set his howdah afire, and this caused his elephant to panic and flee. This produced immediate panic in Dahir's army. The elephant had served the Indian armies well so far. Unfortunately it had no place once gun powder and guns transformed the battle field. India's military failure lay in not recognising this fact and changing its over reliance on the Elephant in time. *The Elephant had become the symbol of royalty and power. It is a regal beast and a majestic mount. So much so that despite its military vulnerabilities, the Central Asian Moghuls nevertheless retained it in their Army as a prize corps.* It was possibly maintained more for its regal symbolism. It is likely that the Mughals innoculated their war elephants to the sound of cannons and explosives. It was the prime means of mobility for a country as vast as India. Its cross country mobility, rate of advance and payload carried was tremendous. However as the explosive paradigm of war proliferated, the Elephant became less and less relevant on the modern battlefield. Slowly it became relegated to the ceremonial and logistic functions. With mechanisation however the day of the elephant is finally over. It has had a long run indeed. It figured first in the pages of the

Mahabharata Epic as a war mount. King Bhagadatta of Kamrupa (modern Assam) was then said to be the greatest Elephant warrior, and soldiers from Kamrupa made the best Elephant troops.

Cohesion of the Ancient Indian Armies

Stephen Peter Rosen in his very analytical book on "Societies and Military Power : India and its Armies," has raised some very pertinent issues. He cites the military theorist Martin Van Creveld to question the existence of such large armies in ancient India. Van Creveld feels that keeping the aspects of logistics (the roads, transport and food storage technology) and command and control aspects in view, the maximum number of troops that could be brought to bear in a battle in those periods of history could be 20,000 only. Hence figures of 650,000 infantry, 8000 chariots, 9000 elephants etc. are gross exaggerations. However Rosen contradicts himself when he compares the Ancient Indian Armies with the Roman Legions. On pp. 95 of his book Rosen cites the peak manpower mobilisation in ancient Rome (Hanibalic wars) as 240,000 from a Roman population base of 2.75 million. Subsequently in the war against the Italian Rebels, the Romans numbered a total of 170,000 troops against Italian rebels numbering 130,000. This amounted to a total military mobilisation of almost 9 per cent of the then Italian population. Ancient India had much higher population levels in the Indo-Gangetic plains and it is mystifying why Rosen seeks to ridicule the figures quoted by Megasthenes and a number of other Greek sources who had little reason to exaggerate Indian military strengths.

The next issue raised by Rosen however is more interesting. How cohesive were these Ancient Indian Armies? How professional were they in the conduct of war? How closely linked were they to the larger Indian polity? Or were they, like the Greek Phalanxes and Roman legions, highly professional forces that had deliberately distanced or insulated themselves from their parent societies. The Phalanxes and Legions had spent many years away from home, engaged in constant warfare. This made them highly professional but also quite insulated and divorced from their parent societies. Rosen feels the ancient Indian Armies were not such highly professionalised micro societies. The Indian polity was highly fragmented on caste and sub-caste divisions. These divisions were mirrored in these Ancient Indian Armies. Thus the Kshatriyas formed the chariot corps and cavalry and rode the elephants. The Vaisyas or cultivators formed the foot Infantry hordes. If this was the case - what was the level of cooperation and coordination between the various Arms of the ancient Indian Armies? How well drilled were they in complex inter arm manoeuvres that combined the Infantry Phalanxes with the Cavalry wings. Rosen cites Alexander's rout of Porus to show that the ancient Indian Armies lacked inter-arm cohesion and coordination. The Greek Phalanxes were highly armoured Infantry that was exceedingly well-drilled and fought (not individually) but as a collective entity. Years of campaigning had made them very professional and very well-coordinated and functionally effective teams. The disjoined Indian responses at the battle of Hydaspas has been used by Rosen to pour scorn on Indian military prowess in that period.

It is again pointed out that Porus was a mere border chieftain. At no stage did Alexander contest the main Indian military power of that era - the Nandas. It must however be conceded that Alexander had enunciated a new and more mobile Paradigm of war that involved long range advances and mobile battles. The Indian Armies of that period were still primed on to massive gladiatorial contests in fixed battle areas which were so selected that the chariots and elephants and infantry and cavalry could be brought to bear in the geometrical formations and battle drills of the Vyuhas. Such a limited Paradigm of attrition was dislocated in the face of a high mobility Paradigm of war that was not confined to fixed battle plains. It was in this cross country mobility that the Indian war chariots - the prize arm of that age were found wanting. Chanakya had come forth to rouse the Indian civilisation against the Greek Invader. Lacking good Cavalry, he correctly analysed the need to shift the Indian Arms emphasis from the chariots to the Elephant Corps. These had matching (if not superior mobility to the Cavalry) and could move cross country. Above all, they exploited the effect of severe psychological shock and were ideal for seige warfare and capturing forts. As recounted earlier, Kautilya used a *brilliant psy war campaign to exploit the shock effect of Indian war elephants on the Greek Armies. This was adequate to cause Alexander to abort his campaign*. Subsequently, when Kautilya's protege Chandragupta Maurya came to power he laid the foundations of a standing and professional Army where the emphasis shifted from Chariots to the elephant Corps as the prime shock arm.

However the Rosen thesis is not entirely without merit. Being inordinately large for that era, the ancient Indian Armies were not perhaps as cohesive and professionalised as the Greek Phalanxes or Roman Legions that had become distinct micro societies in themselves. Apart from the four fold division of the Indian Armies into the four arms we hear (in the *Arthashastra*) of the six fold divisions based upon the type of troops. These included :-

- *The Hereditary Troops (Maula).* These were the hereditary soldiers or Kshatriyas who formed the professional core of the Ancient Indian Armies.
- *Mercenaries (Brhtra).*
- *Guild Levies (Srena).* There were fighting guilds of professional soldiers who sold their services to the king. These were like the Condiotorri of Machieavelle.
- *Soldiers Supplied by Feudatory Chiefs or Allies.* These were called Sruhid Balams
- *Troops Captured or Won Over from the Enemy (Dvisad Balam).* These were not considered very reliable.
- *The Forest Tribes (Atavi-Balam).* These were basically used to plunder the areas through which the Armies advanced. They were regarded as the least reliable of all the six classes of troops.

These six classes of troops indicate how such large force levels were generated in ancient India. Quite obviously the professional cores were small. However we have it on the authority of Megasthenes and others that these were thoroughly professional and well drilled. The others have been listed in their descending orders of reliability. Obviously these conglomerate mixes could not have been as professional or cohesive as the Greek Phalanxes or Roman Legions were. Nevertheless they proved effective enough to defeat the Greek Satrap of Syria and Iran and subsequently stop the Sakas and Huns.

Force Levels

The size of the armies said to have been engaged in the Mahabharata War staggers the imagination. It is said that an overall total of 18 'Akshauhinis' were involved - 11 on the Kaurava side and 7 on the side of the Pandavas. These Akshauhinis are the ancient equivalent of field armies. As per Professor P Sensarma, each Akshauhini was said to have the following :

(a) Chariots	21,870 (each chariot had 5 men)
(b) War elephants	21,870 (each elephant carried 6 men)
(c) Cavalry	65,610
(d) Infantry	109,350

The Akshauhini was a standard field formation and had four types of soldiers based on the four arms :

(a) Ratha	Charioteer
(b) Gaja	Elephant rider
(c) Ashwa	Horse cavalry trooper
(d) Padatee	Foot-soldier (infantrymen)

Based upon this organization the overall strength of the Kaurava and Pandava armies would work out to :

	Ratha	*Gaja*	*Ashwa*	*Padatee*	*Grand total*
Pandavas (7 Akshauhini)	153,090	153,090	459,270	765,450	1,530,900
Kauravas (11 Akshauhini)	240,570	240,570	721,710	1,202,850	2,405,700
Overall Total					3,936,600

Source : Maj P Sensarma, *Kurukshetra War : A Military Study.*

These are mind-boggling figures. One is apt to consider these to be outright exaggerations or poetic hyperbole. However, the same figures have been repeated in the *Dhanurveda,* Kautilya's *Arthashastra* and the *Manu Smriti.* One is apt to question whether at the population levels of these times armies worth 40 lakh regular soldiers could be raised, trained, concentrated in one area and controlled effectively in battle. The Indian mind has a peculiar fascination for mind-boggling, astronomical figures (e.g. the Puranic calculations of the number of years in a Manvantara - age of Manu and Kalpa or day of Brahma etc.). Possibly it is this mathematical penchant for juggling with figures that has led to these astronomical sums. Even the combined strength of the Indian and Pakistani Armed Forced today stands at between 18 to 20 lakhs (including paramilitary forces). So it is debatable whether these old figures are indeed accurate or reliable. However, an Arab proverb says, 'There is no smoke without fire.' That these astronomical figures have been repeated time and again in various ancient Indian texts should itself give an indication that the size of the armies involved was very large.

Records kept by Megasthenes, the Greek Ambassador to the court of Chandragupta Maurya, confirm the presence of a vast and well-organised Mauryan Army running into over six lakhs. Since there is much in common between the *Mahabharata* and Kautilya's *Arthashastra* we may not be able to dismiss the claim of armies running into several lakhs out of hand. Only a war of that magnitude could have such a tenacious hold on the racial memory of the Indian people. To suggest that the Indian civilization *en masse* has been so gullible as to be held in thrall for the past 2500 years by a petty family feud is to insult the intelligence of a people. Such a view needs to be rectified. The figure of 40 lakhs can be dismissed outright as a gross exaggeration but the subsequent Mauryan records would justify the existence of an army at least upto a lakh or more (1.5 to 2 lakhs). VR Mani, another author on the subject, has listed the following armed strength of the Mahabharata War :

(*a*) 21,870 chariots
(*b*) 21,870 elephants
(*c*) 66,610 horses
(*d*) 109,350 infantry

The infantry figures appear more authentic. The figures for chariots and elephants can be reduced by a factor of 10, and those of horses can be reduced by half, on the basis of the known strength of the later Mauryan armies.

Mass Armies

It is interesting to point out that in having the fourth largest army in the world today (the largest volunteer force) we have maintained the ancient Indian tradition of mass, volunteer and professional standing armies that run into several lakhs.

Military Organization

Intelligence is structured in organization. The excellent military organization depicted in the *Mahabharata* speaks volumes of the military wisdom of our ancients. The largest independent field formation in those days, as mentioned earlier, was an Akshauhini. However, the *Dhanurveda* says (*Shlokas* 202-203) that the highest field formations perhaps was an 'army group' called 'Maha Akshauhini' comprising ten Akshauhinis.

Arms

In the *Mahabharata* period there were four basic arms :

(a) *Chariots*. This was the prize arm - equivalent of modern tanks in terms of relative mobility and firepower. Each chariot carried a total of six men and four horses :

• Warrior	One
• Charioteer	One
• Horse keeper	Two
• Flank guards	Two

(b) *Elephants*. The shock arm designed to terrorize the enemy and provide mobility in jungle and even mountainous terrain (upto 12,000 feet). Each war elephant carried six men. The four arms (Chariots, Elephants, Cavalry and Infantry) represent four distinct and variable speed manoeuvre masses. Their integration into cohesive all "Arms teams" and their coordination in the battlefield to execute a common tactical plan, indicate a very high level of sophistications in the art of tactical manoeuvre and better handling of all arms teams. Today, Modern Armies are also divided into four basic arms — Armour, Infantry, Mechanised Infantry and Artillery. The art and science of battle calls for their cohesive employment in all arms teams upon the battlefield. Radio communications have enabled us to coordinate these variable speed manoeuvre masses of the tanks, the Armoured Personal Carriers (or Infantry Combat vehicles) and the classical foot infantry upon the battlefield. Despite the technological sophistication the basic tenets and theory of combined arms manoeuvre would remain broadly the same. Alexanders Arabella (Penetration) or single Canne (single envelopement) manoeuvers can be executed by horses, elephants, chariots or tanks. That is why there is a lot to learn from a study of the Mahabharata techniques of coordinating and controlling variable speed manoeuvre masses on the battlefield. This may turnout to be possibally the most useful and instructive portions of the Mahabharata epic which modern day soldiers could study with immense profit. In the ancient period each elephant was said to have :

• Drivers	Two
• Archers	Two
• Banner holder	One
• Shaktidhari	One

(c) *Horse cavalry* with one rider, each armed with sword, lance and possibly bows and arrows.
(d) *Infantry* which gave flank protection, held ground and bore the brunt of the fighting in terrain where the other three arms could not operate.

It is interesting to note that the Greek Army of Alexander had only two basic arms - infantry and cavalry. The Egyptian armies had infantry, archers and charioteers only. This four arm concept *(Chaturangi)* was an improvement on the Vedic Aryan armies that had only chariots and infantry.

All-Arms Teams

It is interesting to note that each Akshauhini had well-balanced components of all four arms functioning under a single commander (Senapati). In coming to this sytem therefore, India can claim to have beaten Europe (where Napoleon introduced it in the seventeenth century) by over 2000 years! Recently (especially after the October 1973 Yom Kippur War) there has been a lot of talk of the homogenous 'all-arms team' concept. It appears that the organization of the Akshauhini was not rigid but flexible and varied to suit the requirement of a particular *vyuha* or battle formation. This makes it more akin to the Israeli Ugdah or 'Task Force'.

Triangular Organizational Pattern

Theoretically each Akshauhini of 218,700 soldiers comprised ten Aneekinis. Each Aneekini in turn was composed of 3 Camu of 7290 and so on down till the section level called Patti. The table gives the broad organization along with its modern equivalents.

Unit	*Strength*	*Modern equivalent with approximate strength*
Patti	10 men	Section (10 men)
Sena Mukha	30 men	Platoon (30 men)
Gulma	90 men	Company (115 men)
Gana	270 men	Battalion (1000 men)
Vahini	810 men	Brigade (4500 men)
Pritna	2430 men	Division (20,000 men)
Caṃu	7290 men	Corps (30,000 men)
Aneekini	21,870 men	Field Army (100,000 men)

As mentioned earlier, the triangular organization pattern was followed till the level of the Aneekini (field army). Thereafter 10 Aneekinis made the gigantic Akshauhini or army group. The *Dhanurveda* also speaks of a Maha Akshauhini or a 'Super Army Group' of ten such army groups!

Homogeneous All Arms Concept

At this stage we come across a very interesting fact. It is claimed that *down to the section level all arms were represented in each Patti*. Thus it is said that one Patti had the following :

(*a*) One Ratha
(*b*) One Gaja
(*c*) Three Ashwa
(*d*) Five Paditee (making a total of ten).

However this leaves considerable room for confusion. If the figures represent men of various arms then apparently they could not have fought together - but gone to different chariots or elephants. However if they represented one chariot (six men), one elephant (six men), three horses (three men), and five infantry it would lead to a total of 20 men in the basic fighting unit, Patti. *This would, as is apparent, represent the ultimate in achieving homogeneity in a combined arms team.* In most modern armies we have not achieved all-arms integration below the brigade level (armoured brigades of two armoured battalions or regiments and one mechanized infantry battalion and supporting tracked artillery component). Efforts are being made in some armies (French and Swedish) to get this integration down to the battalion level, but to have it down to the squad or platoon level sounds utopian even in todays advanced context.

Triangular Pattern and All-Arms Team concept

These are two organizational principles of the *Mahabharata* era that have apparently stood the test of time and are with us to this day.

Organization for Higher Direction of War

The supreme commanders of the Kaurava and Pandava armies were the kings, i.e. Yudhisthira and Duryodhana, the political heads of state, who occupied the apex of the organizational pyramid. The further chain of command was as under :

(a) *Senapati Pati (Commander-in-Chief).* On the Pandavas' side this post was held by Arjuna. An interesting feature is that the commander-in-chief was not appointed but *elected* by the allied kings from amongst themselves. This democratic process served to prevent friction and personality clashes. Arjuna remained the C-in-C Pandava army right through, whereas the Kaurava army changed five Cs-in-C in the 18-day war. The Mahabharata reveals elaborate procedures to reduce the friction inherent in coalition's warfare. Election of a Supreme commander for battle was one such methodology.

(b) *A Chief of Staff.* The Chief of Staff or advisory functions seem to have been performed by the legendary Krishna. However, he is the sole example. There does not seem to have been a regular staff cadre - except the other chariot drivers who guided their chariot (car) warriors.

(c) *Sarba Senapati (Chief of Generals?).* This post was held by Dhristadyumna in the Pandava army and was superior in status to the Senapati's who commanded an Akshauhini or field army each.

(d) *Senapati (Field Army Commander)* held direct command of the Akshauhinis. Thus the Pandavas had a total of seven Akshauhinis, each under one Senapati. The personages were Drupada, Birata, Styaki, Dhristadyumna (Chief Field Army Commander in addition to his own duties), Dhrishtaketu, Sikhandi and Sahadeva. The Kaurava Senapatis are not clearly enumerated.

The authenticity of such vast numbers in the ancient Armies is highly debatable. However it does point to a refinement of the concept of large standing armies. A large number of these details have been quoted from Major P. Sensarma's book purely for academic interest. Their historic authenticity is difficult to establish. However, even if these are regarded as fiction, they represent the literature of those times and that must surely reflect the level of societal development and sophistication. The existance of these concept of all arms integrations in such ancient texts itself is surprising and serves to highlight the sophistication of the Art of War in the Mahabharata period and beyond in Indian History.

In conclusion the following is pertinent :

(*a*) In the Early Vedic period, Indian Armies had two arms — Infantry and Chariots.

(*b*) By the time of the Mahabharata war (1450 to 900 BC the late Vedic period), we hear of armies with four arms — Chariots, Cavalry, Infantry and Elephants.

(*c*) By the time of Kautilya (Third century BC) the emphasis had shifted from chariots, as the prize arm, to elephants as the main shock arm and instrument of military mobility.

8

Vyuhas : Racial Motifs of War

The *Vyuha* concept is the most revolutionary and characteristically Indian concept of the *Mahabharata*. This forms the watershed of the development of Indian military thought and is peculiar to the Indian psyche and military genius. It is the author's contention that it is this which holds a great deal of relevance for us today, especially in the field of mechanized operations.

What is a Vyuha?

Normally a *Vyuha* is taken to mean a simple formation adopted by an army or its subunits to fight a particular battle. But a *Vyuha* went a little beyond that. The geometrical organization of the *Vyuha* restricted the tactical options open to the enemy to a few predictable responses. These were catered for by well-rehearsed battle drills. To elucidate, let us say one army adopted a circular formation or *Vyuha*. Then to attack it the enemy had a limited set of options. These were treated as contingencies for which detailed battle drills were laid down. That implies that ancient Indian military leaders did not rely on conventional appreciations - but to ensure

- speed of decision
- elimination of confusion, and
- minimal wastage of time in passage of orders

relied upon well-laid set of battle drills which were integral to each battle formation or *Vyuha*. The Mahabharata epic mentions a large number of Vyuhas. These were either based on geometrical shapes or animal forms. Thus we had circular, half-moon or crescent shaped, square shaped and

Needle point Vyuhas in the former category. In the latter there were Vyuha formation based on the shapes of Herons, Vultures, Eagles or like a whale or fish. Each Vyuha was not just a geometrical shape or array. It also had its set piece battle drills. The conceptualisation of Vyuhas was possibly aided by representative games like chess or chausar. It is said that a Brahmin devised the Indian game of chess. It was essentially a wargame. The chess board represented the battlefield and the horses, footsoldiers and elephants were the chess pieces. Representative wargames like there must have been instrumental in the development of Vyuha battle arrays and battledrills. These helped to synchronise and harmonise the actions of four variable speed manoeuvre masses on the battlefield. The battle arrays and their associated battle drills helped to reduce the fog and friction of war and unleashed coherent and controlled responses to set piece situations.

Soviet Vyuhas?

It is interesting to note that the erstwhile Soviet Army used to advocate a similar methodology. In the Red Army there were no conventional 'appreciations'. Below divisional levels, brigades and battalions and below fought as per well-rehearsed and thoroughly understood battle drills. True, to some extent it might curb initiative, but this method is most suitable for the flux and confusion of fast-moving, mechanized battles. That is why an army, as professional and competent as the erstwhile Soviet Army, placed great reliance on well-practised battle drills to cater for the likely contingencies that can easily be foreseen in peacetime. The Soviets called it the concept of standard norms. The tactical commander trains against standard norms in repetitive drills; he applies them to solve tactical problems in the field. He uses them for measuring training progress, determining rates of march and advance, developing the number of rounds of artillery to be fired against a specific target to accomplish specific results. Colonel V Kashin of the Soviet Army had worked out the following mathematical formula for deriving such norms :

$$N = \frac{1}{n} \sum_{t=1} N_1$$

The value of the base norm of the performance of a combat task can be practically derived as the arithmetical mean of the actual time expenditure for the given task by different units (under different conditions). Units are then graded in these in terms of excellent, good or satisfactory.

Combat Group Battle Drills -
The Secret of Rommel's Success

This battle drill concept has been tried out and has the sanction of history. In fact combat group battle drills were the secret of Rommel's success against far larger and qualitatively superior Allied forces in North Africa in the Second World War.

An analysis of the force levels indicates that Rommel, in overall numerical terms, was far inferior to the British throughout the campaign. Was his success due then to the qualitative superiority of his equipment? BH Liddell Hart in his *History of the Second World War* has dealt exhaustively with this aspect. Analysing the technical factor while discussing the British defeat at Gazala he says :

> "Most of the German medium tanks were armed with the short 50 mm gun - which had a penetration slightly inferior to the 2 pounder gun of high muzzle velocity with which all the British tanks were armed. In armour most of the German tanks in 1941 had been more thinly protected than the newer British Cruisers (30 mm max against 40 mm). The Grant had 78 mm of armour and the Valentines 65 mm of armour. In anti-tank guns too the British had regained the qualitative advantage through the arrival of their 6-pounder (57 mm) gun which was 30 per cent superior in penetration to the 50 mm anti-tank gun of the Germans. Although the German 88 mm gun still remained the most formidable tank-killer, Rommel had only 48 of these guns and their high mounting made them much more vulnerable than any of the standard anti-tank guns on either side.

Liddell Hart concludes, an analysis of the technical factor provides no adequate explanation of the Eighth Army's defeat at Gazala. The evidence clearly shows that this was due to the Germans' superior tactics in general and especially to their tactical combination of tanks with anti-tank guns.

The Laager (box) Combat Group Battle Drill

Let us now go into details of these superior tactics for they hold the key

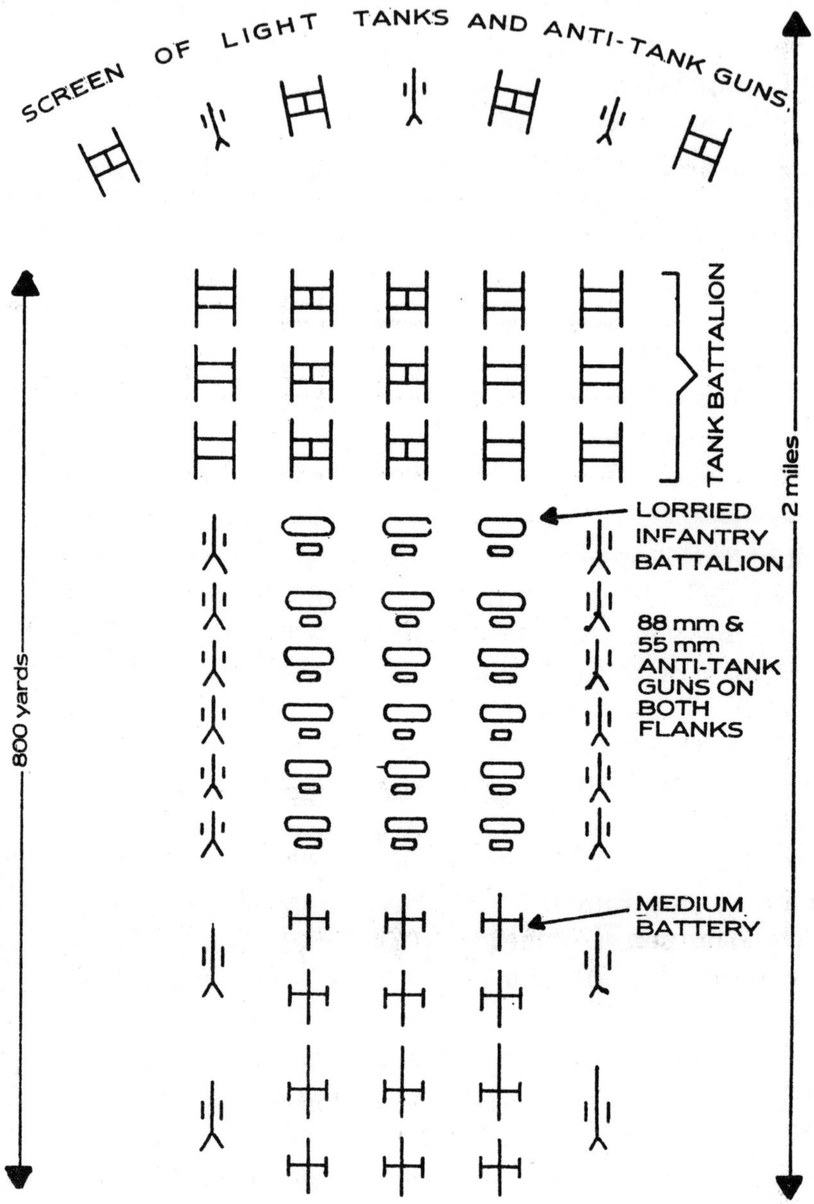

Fig. 8.1 German Laager on The Move

to Rommel's phenomenal success. A prominent feature of this was the German 'Laager' method of fighting. This has been described in detail by Colonel HB Letham in an article that was published in the *Royal Artillery Journal* in 1941. Broadly speaking, when at rest each formation forms an 'anti-tank, square' or a box and when on the move, the unarmoured arms and services march within the square with the armoured formations escorting them. If a German tank battalion was moving it normally had the following grouped with it :

- One Battalion Lorried Infantry.
- One Battery 50 mm Anti-Tank guns.
- One Battery 88 mm AA Guns.
- One Troop 150 mm close support guns.
- One Battery Field Guns.

The entire mobile 'box' or moving Laager formed a square 800 yards wide and 2 miles deep (See Fig. 8.1). The soft lorries of the motorized infantry and other A1 and A2 Echelons' vehicles were placed in a compact group inside the box arranged for immediate all-round defence. The 50 mm and 88 mm anti-tank and anti-aircraft guns were deployed on the outside flanks and front faces of the box. The tanks moved ahead of it in three rows with 50 yards between tanks. A reconnissance element comprising Mk III tanks, heavy machine guns and anti-tank guns moved well ahead of the main 'box' or Laager to provide early warning.

Laager Battle drill

The moment the British armour was contacted by the reconnissance elements (or its presence was reported) the entire 'box' halted and the tanks took up positions on either side of the box — so that the formation looked like a giant 'T' (see Fig. 8.2). The German reconnissance element then began a fighting withdrawal causing delay and casualties to the advancing British armour. This was done primarily by leap-frogging between guns and tanks. The British armour now had three basic options :

- To outflank the box and attack from the right.
- To outflank and attack from left.
- To attack frontally.

Let us say the British armour decided to attack from the left. The tanks of the left arm of the German 'T' fell back to lure the British armour in. As the British tanks pressed forward they were not only engaged frontally by the Mk IV Panzer tanks but also caught in the flanks by the German anti-aircraft and anti-tank guns deployed on the left flank of the box. Finally the tanks on the German right flank (or arm of the 'T') would swing around and attack the British tanks from the rear. The British armour would thus be caught in concentric fire from all three sides (see Fig. 8.3). The same drill could be repeated if the British decided to outflank from the right. If they decided to attack frontally - the German tanks on both flanks of the box would envelop them from both sides. It was this simple but setpiece battle drill using a judicious combination of tanks and anti-tank guns that caught the British armour in concentric fire from three sides time and again.

Even today, such battle drills could ideally be adopted by us in the desert terrain. Slight local variations would be required to relate it to the actual ground/dune configurations but the overall principles if clearly grasped by commanders at all levels (down to the tank troop and mechanized infantry platoon) would lead to quick and meaningful engagements. Our armoured formations would not 'drift' into battle by troops and squadrons with very little centralized control as is normally their wont. We can use anti-tank missiles and recoilless guns to replace the 50 mm and 88 mm German guns.

Even today such combat drills should be known to all personnel and be thoroughly rehearsed so that they can be set into motion with the minimum of orders. They would achieve a very high degree of speed in decision, reaction, issue of orders and their execution. The enemy would be compelled to attack our stationary tanks and anti-tank guns and be liable to encirclement from three sides minimum. It would force the enemy to react to situations created by us. In adopting this battle drill we would be taking a leaf straight out of Rommel's book.

The advantages of such setpiece battle drills over conventional 'mental' appreciations in a mechanized battle setting would be patently obvious to any unbiased observer. More such battle drills can be worked and thoroughly rerhearsed for various situations and settings. These can be tried and constantly improved in the light of experience. Each such battle drill would have a set of built-in contigencies to cater for likely enemy reactions. In the fast-moving timeframe of mechanized operations, drills would have a far

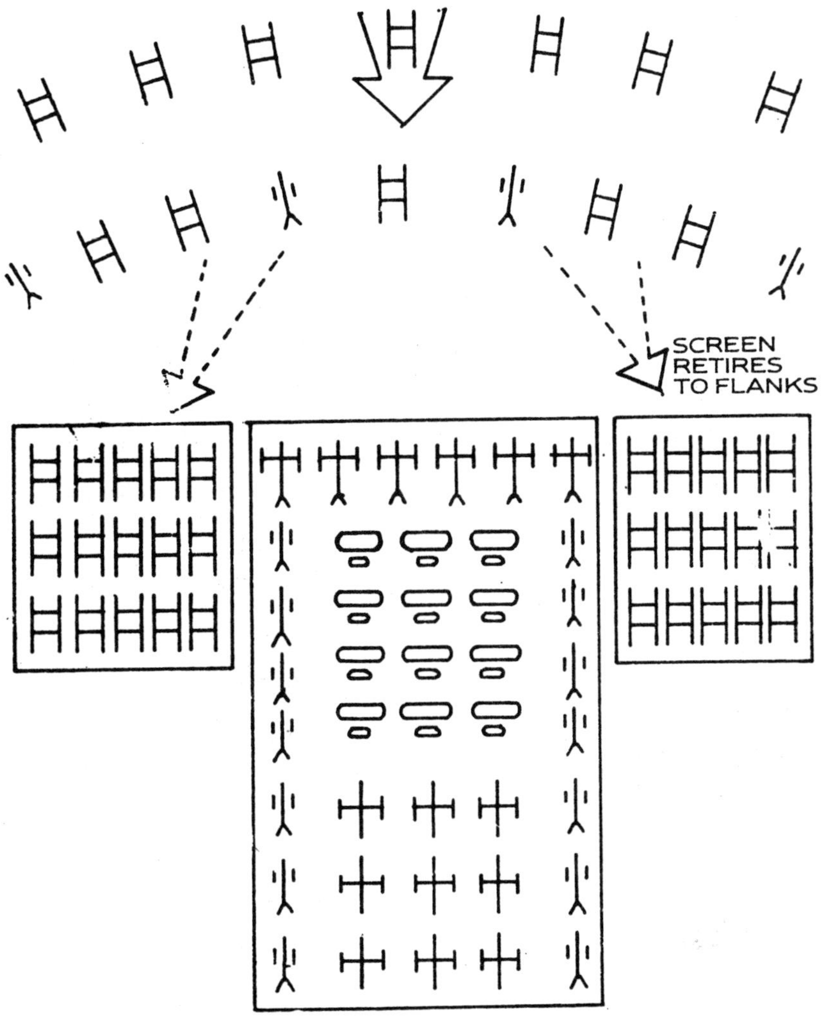

Fig. 8.2 Laager Adopts Defensive Formation as Screen Contacts British Armour

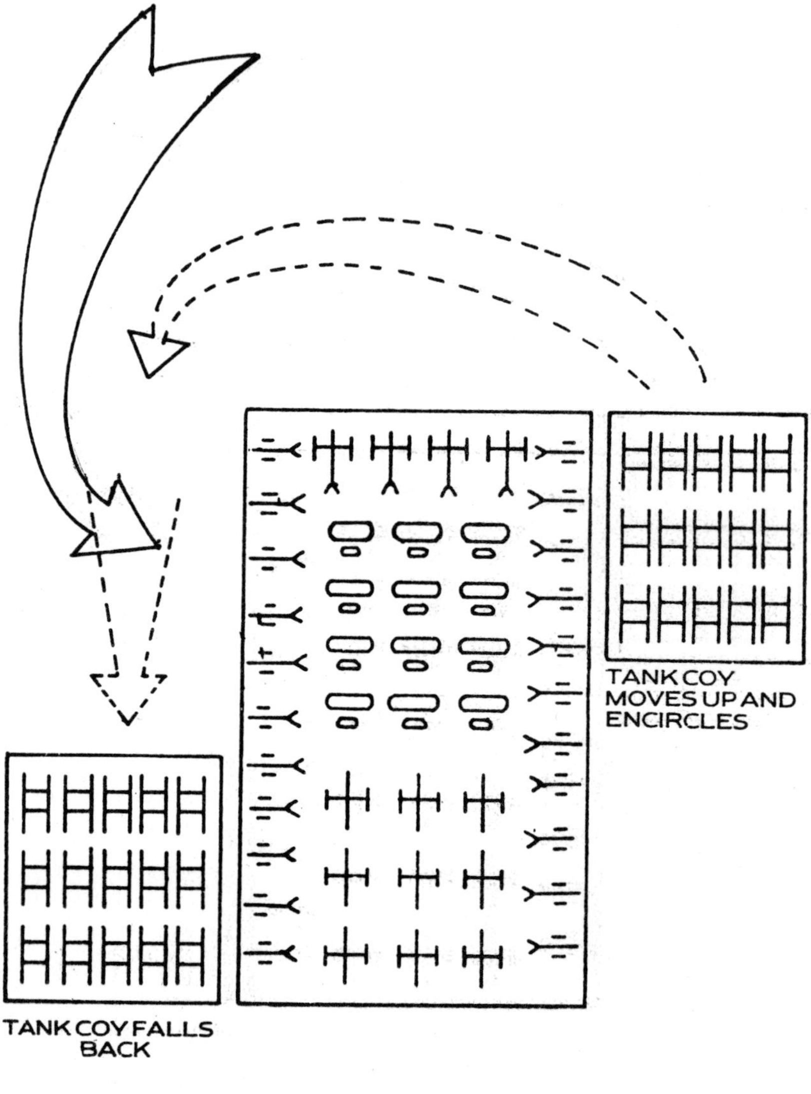

Fig. 8.3 Laager Battle Drill Traps British Flank Attack in Concentric Fire From Three Sides

greater chance of success than solutions produced from tedious process of logical analysis.

We have seen the example of one particular battle drill followed by Rommel's Panzers in Africa. Even today we could work out a whole series of such battle drills pertinent to our requirements. The startling fact is that this laager formation very closely resembles the Shakta Vyuha formation cited in the *Mahabharata*. This was also a T-shaped formation. The soft infantry was placed within the box. The chariots replaced the tanks and formed the head of the 'T'. The similarity is so astounding that it takes one's breath away. The figure at the beginning of the book visually highlights the remarkable similarity in shape and design between the T shaped German Tank Laager and the Shakata Vyuha mentioned in the Mahabharata. In war the basic manoeuvres whether executed by foot infantry, horses or tanks are archetypal. Alexander's Arabella (penetration manoeuvre) or the single or double 'Canne' is still executed by armoured columns. Hannibal's Arabella manoeuvre also lends itself to emulation by a modern mechanized force. Art forms in war are archetypal. The Indian *Vyuhas* need to be studied in this light.

VYUHAS – INDIANIZED METHOD OF BATTLE

Every people have their own characteristic genius and racial patterns of waging war. Success can best be obtained by fighting in conformity with these racial patterns. The shock of combat leads to confusion and disorder. When larger mechanized formations collide on the battlefield, the use of well-rehearsed battle drills will ensure that the disintegration caused by combat is along prescribed and thought-out patterns. Just as crystals crystallize in a particular way for various chemicals so also mechanized formations should shake out into particularized battle formations with built-in contingency drills when under the shock of combat. This 'crystal formation', should be as automatic as the chemical process alluded to.

A brief glance at Indian military history and our epics and treatises on warfare like the *Mahabharata*, the *Arthashastra*, the *Sadashiva Dhanurveda*, the *Shukra Niti* and to some extent the *Puranas* — all confirm the Indian concept of fighting in *Vyuhas*. Innumerable such *Vyuhas* like *Chakravyuha*, *Bajra Vyuha*, *Suchi Mukha Vyuha*, *Ardhachandra Vyuha*, etc. are mentioned. These were not just battle formations but battle formations with set battle drills for a set of likely contingencies very much like the German Laager method quoted earlier. If that is so, in falling back upon such Laager-type battle drills we will be taking recourse to a very ancient Indian method of waging war — a methodology that is part of our myth and racial memory. It is intimately suited to our genius and, if applied on the battlefield, would lead to success.

There is a need to formulate a style and method of war that is Indian in conception and context, that suits our needs and genius, and is ideal for our peculiar combat requirements. The reintroduction of the Indian concept of *Vyuhas* or particularized battle drills would be one such step towards this end.

The resurrection of the battle drills (*Vyuha*) concept as opposed to the 'Appreciation' concept of arriving at combat decision could lead to the revival of a wholly Indian form of war. Just as art forms and motifs are constant for a people, so are the forms of war.

Mechanics of Vyuhas

I have dwelt at length on the German Laager, for this, in essence, explains the working of the *Vyuha* system. It is interesting to note the startling similarity between the German Laager formation and the *Shakta Vyuha* (T-formation which placed cavalry on both flanks) of the *Mahabharata*. Thus a *Vyuha* was not only a particular geometrical layout of the arms of the army but also comprised set battle drills based upon likely enemy reactions to that formation.

Types of Vyuhas

Many types of *Vyuha* are mentioned in the *Mahabharata*. They can broadly be classified under two heads :

(a) *Those based on geometrical figures, for example :*

- *Sarbatomukha Vyuha* and *Chakravyuha* and *Mardalu Vyuha*. Circular formation.
- *Aradhchandra Vyuha*. Crescent formation.
- *Shakta Vyuha and Bajra Vyuha*. T-shaped formation.
- *Sagara Vyuha*. Square formation.
- *Suchi Mukha Vyuha*. Needle head formation.

(b) *Those based on animal archetypal shapes :*

- *Garura Vyuha* - Shaped like an eagle.
- *Makara Vyuha* - Shaped like a fish or whale.
- *Krauncha Vyuha* - Shaped like a heron.
- *Syena Vyuha* - Shaped like a vulture.

There were many combination shapes, e.g. Chakra-Shakta Vyuha which was a combination of the Chakravyuha (circular formation) and Shakta Vyuha (T-shaped formation).

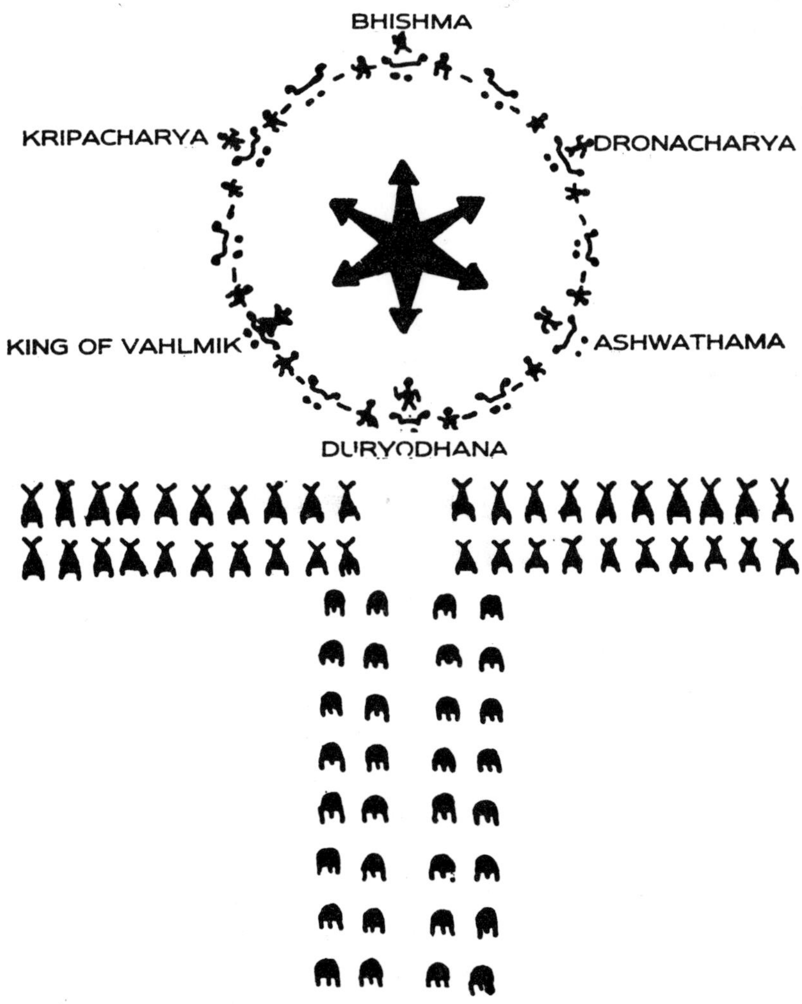

Fig. 8.4 Sarbatomukha Vyuha

Parts of Vyuha

The parts of a *Vyuha* have been described by Brihaspati as :

(a) *Paksha* (two) - Two wings in the front.
(b) *Urasva* - the centre.
(c) *Pratigraha* - The Rear.
(d) *Kaksha* (two) - Two wings at the rear.

These parts in the main show the concern for flank and rear protection.

Relevance to Modern Conditions

The following *Vyuha* can be deemed relevant even in the modern context :

(a) *Chakra* or *Sarbatomukha Vyuha*. The circular formation that affords all-round defence (sited for all-round defence). Very akin to perimeter defence or defence adopted in jungles or desert terrain (see Fig. 8.4).

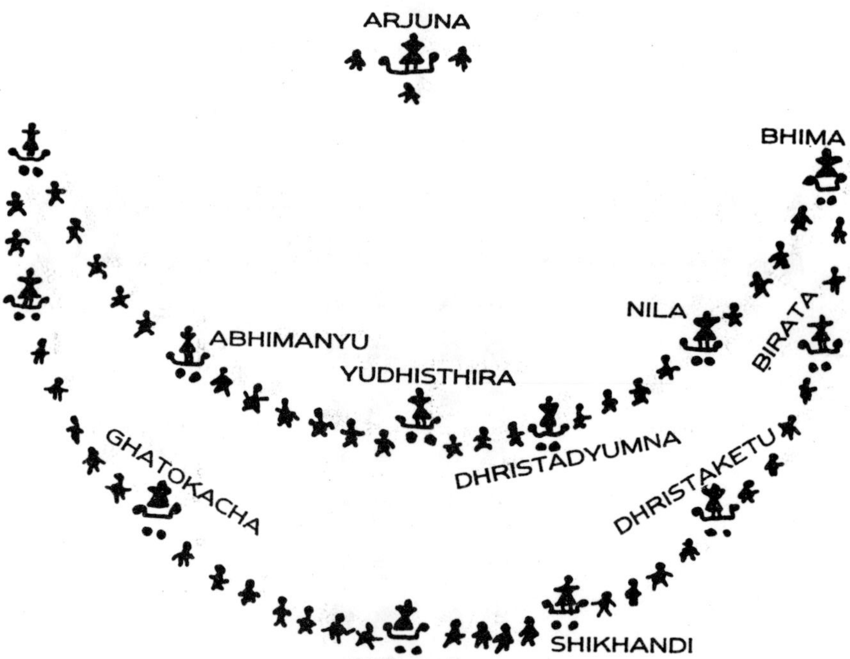

Fig. 8.5 Ardhachandra Vyuha

(b) *Ardha Chandra Vyuha*. Crescent-shaped (half moon) formation primarily employed for defence. This is very similar in pattern to the horse-shoe shaped deployment that we used in the Battle of Asal Uttar in the 1965 Indo-Pak War (see Fig. 8.5).

(c) *Shakta* or *Bajra Vyuha*. T-shaped formation (see Fig. 8.6) so surprisingly similar to stage two of the German Laager formation of the Second World War. This was an offensive-defensive formation — very suitable for advance into enemy territory.

(d) *Suchi Mukha* or *Makara Vyuha*. Needle head or whale shaped formation. This is excellent for launching an attack at a particular weak spot in great depth (see Fig. 8.7). This would be analogous to a deep penetration by armour at a pre-selected 'Schwerpunkt' or thrust point. In the Second World War the Germans concentrated ten Panzer Divisions in the Ardennes for their invasion of France. Such a phalanx of armour arranged in such depth over a narrow frontage would look like a gigantic whale if viewed from above.

Combat Decision-Making — The Psychological Aspects

Perhaps, we need to look more deeply into the psychological mechanics of the process of decision-making on the battlefield. The Indian Army's tactical methodology as inherited from the British lays great emphasis on the process of military appreciation of the situation. This is a highly contrived and laboured process of a step by step, logical analysis. Neurophysiologists tell us that the human brain has two lobes (hemispheres) — the left lobe and the right lobe. The left deals with processes of linear-sequential logic and the right with holistic functions (or Gestalt-like) vision. To give an example of holistic functions once you enter a room you do not perceive it as such by a mental process of 'four walls + two doors + two windows + ceiling + furniture = room'. Rather you perceive the 'whole room' first and then proceed to examine its individual components. From the psychological point of view, all staff work would be a left lobe function — while all command decision functions would be performed by the right lobe of the brain. The command decision in the battlefield has perforce to be a holistic function if it is to proceed with due speed. This implies that all the underlying codes of the 'Tactical Grammar' must be part of the subconscious and operate at that level in an automatic fashion to help in the formulation of workable tactical

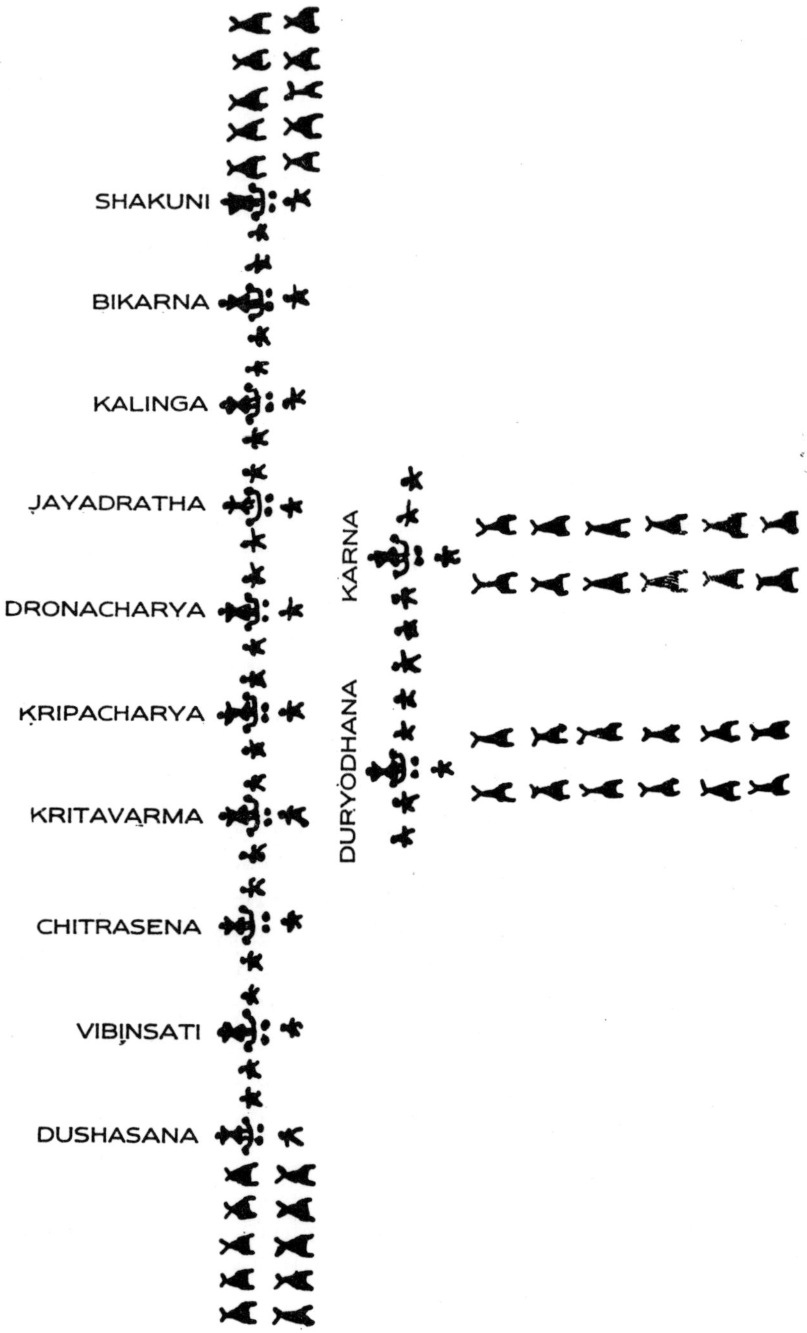

Fig. 8.6 Shakta Vyuha

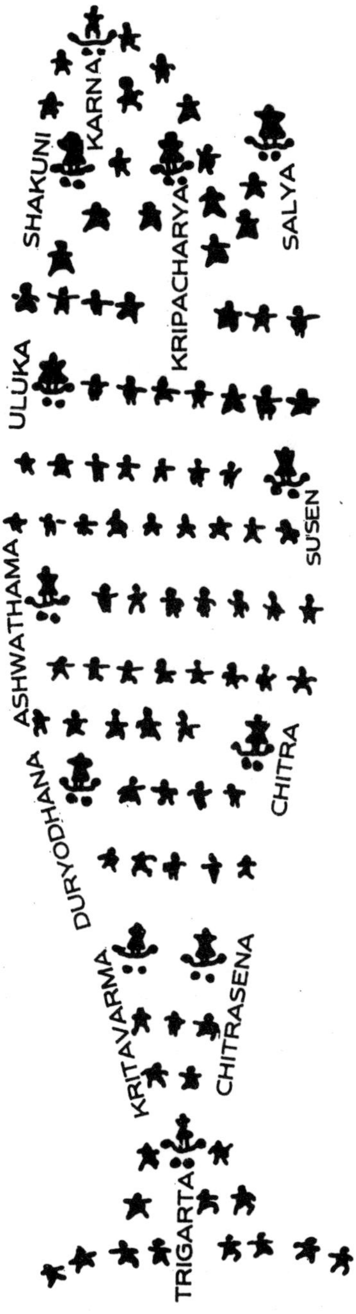

Fig. 8.7 Makara Vyuha

solutions. The command decision would be a Gestalt, a 'holistic flash', rather than a laborious and tediously contrived process of a step-by-step logical analysis. The modern battlefield will not permit its commanders the luxury of such slow analytical process. If that is so why don't Armies alter the thrust of their tactical training and de-emphasize the 'Appreciation' technique of coming to a decision?

Let me clarify further. In the process of appreciating a tactical situation we take each factor by itself and view it in isolation. This is the process that gives us the cause-effect relationship that leads us to the solution. In neuro-psychological terms you are now following a linear — sequential — logical chain. This is the function of the left lobe of the brain which is *not* the seat of decision-making. You are thus using the wrong neurological tool for the wrong job. Staff work is a natural left lobe function — command decision is *not*. For it is the right lobe of the brain which has the capability for holistic appraisal, i.e. it automatically views each factor not in isolation but as part of the 'whole picture'. The resultant Gestalt is much faster. This is also the seat of creativity. In the right lobe not only can you go speedily along straight line chains of logic but also 'leap sideways' to new and brilliant solutions. In following our present appreciation methodology we are reducing our commanders to staff officers. We are allowing trivial and non-essential details of minor SD (Staff Duties) to cramp his style and speed of decision-making. We are, in effect, ensuring that nothing new, original or creative can ever result from such a cramped process. Our solutions no wonder are hackneyed, lack-lustre and predictable.

The Role of Memory

It is very important to understand the role of memory in decision-making. Whenever you analyse a problem you unconsciously view it against a frame of your past experience of similar situations. Obviously your reaction will be much faster if you can recognize the similarities of the present situation with a problem that you have already solved earlier. This 'recognition' is also a holistic function. Another factor must be kept in mind. Memory or recall normally follows the chain association method. Facts are easily remembered if they are arranged in a logical cause-effect relationship. Just one cue is then required to retrieve a whole chain of associated facts.

Let us now apply this knowledge to the solution of tactical problems. To enable a speedy subconscious analysis it would be essential to develop a holistic process. One such method would be to derive 'tactical-templates' which are committed to memory. Any battlefield situation can quickly be viewed in terms of these subconscious tactical templates. The moment you recognize a 'similarity' you can at once unleash a learnt response. In simpler terms it would mean :

(a) For any given tactical problem at the unit/subunit level there are normally two or three set responses — which can be derived from a study of past military operations and the effect of new weapon systems, if any.

(b) These should be thoroughly understood and memorized so that they become a part of an unconscious process.

(c) The response to a similar tactical situation on the battlefield can be :

- Any one of the 'set responses' committed to memory.
- A speedy permutation or combination of the responses so learnt keeping in mind the peculiarities of the present situation.

All those who play chess know that good players have memorized some set opening 'gambits' or a series of moves that set the pace for the rest of the game, and force it to follow a more or less predictable pattern. The author is advocating the learning of such tactical moves or 'opening gambits' for likely tactical situations that can be encountered on the battlefield. The commander must be trained to take a 'holistic' view of the battlefield (which is not difficult since vision itself is a holistic function) — then quickly decide as to which 'learnt response' he wishes to use. This will:

(a) reduce the time for decision-making.

(b) reduce the confusion on the battlefield by producing predictable situations (for us — not the enemy).

(c) increase the speed in execution by lower sub-units who are well rehearsed in the relevant battle drills.

Protagonists of the logical process will protest that this will curb initiative and make our actions predictable. I would like to point out that our appreciations today are more stereotyped and predictable whereas memorized tactical moves can lead to a quick and creative permutation or combinations on the battlefield. Chess has not become a boring game just because Grand Masters have almost comitted to memory certain set 'game strategies'. 'Situating the Appreciations' perhaps is not really as silly as it is made to sound.

The ancient Indian art of war placed great emphasis on the theory and practice of such *Vyuhas* or battle drills. These battle drills represent the Indian genius for war and deserve to be studied in very great detail. In this chapter I have tried to show in detail exactly what the ancient Indian concept of Vyuha represented. It was not only a battle formation or geometrical array. It also involved a set of well practised battle drills or procedures for executing a given task. It served to coordinate the actions of the four different manoeuvre masses of the chariots, the elephants, the cavalry and the infantry on a given battle field. This manoeuvre was coordinated as per a precise plan to achieve given results. This served to reduce the fog and friction of war. The Germans and Russian have used similar batter drills in recent military history. We have a great deal to learn from the theory and practise of Vyuhas. This may be the most useful and instructive portion of the Mahabharata for it deals with combined or All Arms maneuvres and integration upon a fluid and fast-moving battlefield.

Acknowledgement Sketches of Vyuhas have been taken from Professor P. Sensarma's book *Kurukshetra War : A Military Study.*

9

Attrition versus Mobility : The Transition from Mahabharata to Kautilya

Doctrinal Analysis

In purely doctrinal terms, therefore, the Mahabharata epic represents an attritional paradigm of war that is central to the Indian Military tradition (as enshrined in the Mahabharata). It was a military paradigm that laid emphasis on annihilation and destruction of the enemy forces in a pure "force on force" regime. The ancient Indian Armies we encounter in the Mahabharata are huge and ponderous organisations. There is a core of well-drilled regular troops whose numbers are possibly vastly enhanced by the addition of irregular levies (especially in the ranks of the Infantry and Cavalry). Though later Indian texts speak of six classes of troops (Hereditary professionals, fighting guilds, mercenaries, allied troops, enemy troops won over, and forest tribes), the Mahabharata seems to refer to large standing armies which were exceptionally well drilled in combined arms operations and fighting in Vyuhas or standard battle arrays with a specified set of battle drills that catered for likely enemy responses. Each Vyuha (or geometrical battle array) was countered or broken by a well thought out counter array. Thus a Chakra Vyuha or a circular battle array could be defeated by the Suchi Mukha Vyuha (Needle point array) that focussed on a particular weak spot and caused a penetration by massing successive waves of troops on a narrow frontage at the selected thrust point (needle point). Not only were these Vyuhas mere geometrical formations in which the various arms of the armies were arrayed for battle, but each vyuha had also, inherent in itself, a set of battle drills or battle procedures that were well rehearsed and initiated automatically by simple conch/flag/drum signals. These battle drills were like the opening gambits of a chess grand master- well learnt by rote by the commanders and troops and executed with automatic precision on the battlefield. These battle drills were designed to reduce the fog and friction of war and impose order on the battlefield and shape it in accordance with a well-thought out design. Such a level of precision battle manoeuvre is surprising for armies of this antiquity. The Mahabharata, however, is full of the descriptions of varied Vyuhas and their counter Vyuhas adopted by the two sides on each day of the battle. The Geometrical battle arrays and their associated battle drills were designed as "kill-drills" to systematize the process of attrition on the battlefield. What is of profound interest is the fact that these battle arrays and battle drills seek to synthesize and coordinate the actions of four different manoeuvre masses on the battlefield.

- The prize arm of the Chariots
- The shock arm of the Elephant Corps
- The Horsed Cavalry
- The slowest maneuver mass of the Infantry (which is generally described as taking the most horrendous casualties at the hands of the faster paced arms)

Martin Van Crevalds doubts on the ability of the ancient armies to focus resources for meaningful tactical and operational manoeuvre on the designated battlefield are belied by the detailed descriptions in the Mahabharata epic of commanders overseeing the adoption of a given Vyuha on horseback by touring their armies literally for miles before the commencement of battle. Apparently drum, flag and conch signals sufficed to convey instructions to well-drilled troops who had apparently rehearsed such arrays and battle drills to perfection in peacetime. Coordinating and synergising the actions of four different arms (comprising four distinct manoeuvre masses moving at varying speeds) speaks volumes of the sophistication of the art of war in those ancient times. Possibly these highly sophisticated manoeuvre were perfected by representative wargames like chess or *Chauser*, which helped the ancient grandmasters to conceptualize such intricate moves and battle-drills.

This tactical sophistication, however, was possibly its own undoing. Such complex orchestration of variable speed manoeuvre masses was possible only in very limited number of battlefields that were flat and open and had good visibility. Such sophisticated, all arms tactical manoeuvre would perforce be limited by the range of audibility/visibility of the means of signaling (flags, conches, drums etc) available in those times. These limitations in turn engineered the Attrition oriented style of war fighting in predesignated battle plains that became massive gladiatorial combats of force on force. The armies rested by night and fought by day. They adopted a given battle array that by and large dictated the course of the days combat. The rest was highly dependent upon the individual skill of the car warriors and elephant troops. The Indian horsed cavalry was not a very efficient fighting platform (in the absence of stirrups and bits). The entire aim of the exercise was pure and simple annihilation and destruction of the enemy force in a painful "meat grinder war" that could be efficiently fought only on such pre-designated battle plains. Sophistication at tactical manoeuvre and coordination of variable speed manoeuvre masses was only possible in such restricted battle plains. The prize arm of that era- the war chariot was custom built for combat on such flat and open surfaces. It painfully lacked cross-country mobility. The elephants were far more mobile. They were the favourite war mounts of the troops of the Eastern parts of the country (especially of Kamrupa — modern day Assam. An Assamese king Bhagadatta was reputedly the greatest Elephant warrior of that era). *The liet motif of the Mahabharatan style of war was attrition, annihilation and destruction.* Battle arrays and tactical battle drills for precision manoeuvre of all arms in a well-defined battle plain were all designed to facilitate the attrition process. The two armies would fight on till one wore the other down by means of sheer attrition. In later years the contest was often decided in a single day's battle when the other side just disintegrated, lost cohesion and fled. It usually suffered its worst losses while in flight. This force on force Mahabharatan Paradigm of Attrition therefore, is our primal civilisational inheritance. Brilliance at tactical precision maneuver and battle drills however was unfortunately not matched by clarity at the operational and strategic levels of military art. The primitiveness of the means of command, control and communications of that age inherently imposed the limitation. Within these limitations, however, the ancient Indian armies nevertheless displayed a surprising degree of sophistication in tactical manoeuvre in a limited battle area and in coordinating the actions of four variable speed manoeuvre masses of the Chariots, the Elephants, the Cavalry and the Infantry. This tactical oversophistication however was sadly not matched by brilliance at the operational and strategic levels of military art.

The Shock of Encountering the Greek Mobility Paradigm

The Mahabharatan style four armed (*Chaturangi*) armies formed the basic format of the Indian armies not only of that era but down till the 10th century AD. Indian armies changed little in form, content and battle drills for well over 1500 years. These were ponderous; attrition oriented armies, designed to perform at their best in a flat open area. They were not primed for mobile warfare and cross-country movement. The first shock that the Indian military system received was as a result of its collision with the Mobility Paradigm perfected by the Greeks of Alexander. Alexander led campaigns that were excellent at the level of strategic and operational Art. His Greek phalanxes and Cavalry had been well drilled in tactical execution over years of non-stop combat and consequent on the job training in the wars of the Greek City states. The sheer mobility of Alexander's hotly contested advances from Greece, on to Asia-Minor, through Persia and Central Asia into Afghanistan and finally bursting into the Indo-Gangetic flood plains of the Sub-Continent, is a remarkable exercise in Strategic and Operational Mobility. Alexander's emphasis on manoeuvre led to a style of war that was not premised on engagements only in specified battle plains. These could occur anywhere. Alexander often sought to surprise his opponents by advancing through seemingly impassable terrain. In the Battle of Hydaspes both armies were arrayed across the river Jhelum. Alexander marched and counter marched up and down the river several times in feints aimed at distracting the Indians. Then he effected a surprise crossing down stream. The Indian Chariots painfully lacked cross-country mobility. In the wet, marshy river margins they bogged down badly. Since the command elements rode in the chariots, the cohesion of the Indian manoeuvre mass was disrupted even before the onset of battle. After this encounter crossing, Porus's army gave a better account of itself in a set piece battle- largely on account of the shock effect of its corps of elephants. Even here the well drilled Greek phalanxes and Cavalry had the betfer of the Indians. The Indian Attrition Paradigm was floundering in the face of the Greek mobility paradigm. The legendary Kautilya carefully studied the early battles with the Greeks. He realised the relative ineffectiveness of the Indian chariots for mobile warfare. Its cross-country mobility was severely restricted. He was equally quick to note the shock effect of the Indian Elephant Corps on Greek morale. The Elephant was a totally new weapon system for the Greeks and it terrified them. New weapon systems often have an initial impact that is far greater than their actual combat effectiveness. This shock effect takes some time to wear off. Kautilya used this shock effect to weave brilliant psywar themes that caused a conquering Greek Army to halt in its tracks and mutiny. Kautilya therefore transformed the purely attrition-oriented paradigm of the Mahabharatan era into a far more mobile paradigm. He went a step ahead of the Greeks in his advocacy of the Indirect Approach. *Kautilya is the world's first master of Information warfare*. His first priority was to gain information dominance by getting to know more and more about the enemy and at the same time by influencing and shaping his perceptions and responses by the skillful manipulation of information that was fed to him. Kautilya's psychological warfare campaign exploiting the shock effect of the war Elephant (a radically new weapon system for the Greeks) has few parallels in world military history. Kautilya therefore made a significant modification to the basal Mahabharatan Paradigm that was premised on pure attrition.

- The Chariots the prize arm of the Mahabharatan period was phased out.
- Elephants became the prime shock arm. A Sanskrit proverb aptly summed it up by saying, "Where there are Elephants, there is Victory".
- The four-armed (*Chaturangi*) Paradigm therefore gave way to the three-armed organizational structure of later Indian Armies that comprised Elephants, Cavalry and Infantry. The Chariots went into disuse and disappeared from the Sub-continental battlefields.
- The greatest change however was in strategic emphasis. The prime target was now the mind of the enemy commander and through him that of his troops in the field.
- Much in line with the maxim of Sun Tzu, force became a last resort option and the use of Force without war acquired increasing primacy.
- For its antiquity and age the Mauryan military machine was the world's first armed forces to lay such overwhelming emphasis on information dominance and intelligence operations. A vast army of spies (legal, illegal and others) was used to acquire information about

every aspect of the enemy state. Intelligence operations were employed to overthrow the enemy state without the use of force if possible and if not, by using force only as a final coup de grace that exploited a very skillful information- warfare and covert action campaign aimed at destabilising and imbalancing the target state.

The Primacy of Economics

It is difficult to appreciate the surprising degree of sophistication in statecraft that had been achieved in the times of Kautilya. The degree of sophistication displayed was simply remarkable for that era. The Kautilyan State clearly gave primacy to Economics over military might. Kautilya said, "of the *Kosha* (*Treasury*) and the *Danda* (*military machine*) the Treasury is more important". War was therefore not an end in itself. It served to enhance the economic power of the state and expand its territories and areas of tribute. Present day theorists of geo-economics would have a lot to learn from Kautilya. War and overt conflict were usually his option of last resort. He relied more upon skillful information war campaigns to destabilize and weaken his king's opponents and enemies. He used spies and saboteurs to subvert and to sow dissension and discord; to create dissonance and to destabilize. Military force was used most economically, often only as a swift coup de grace that came as the culmination of a long covert campaign of destabilisation. *The destruction of the geo political and military balance of a state was an essential precursor to a physical attack.* Psychological war and covert operations had perforce to precede a conventional coup de grace. War was never an end in itself- it was a means for the state to enhance its power and prestige and the primal basis of the states activities was purely economic. The present-day Indian state has continued to give primacy to economics over warfighting. India still spends amongst the world's lowest percentage of its GDP on defence. However, by sheer force of historical habit, our military echelons unconsciously seem to regress time and again from the Mobility Paradigm of Kautilya to the more primal Attrition Paradigm of the Mahabharata (with its emphasis on Chivalry and direct force on force engagements). It is an inheritance that is too deeply ingrained to be forgotten easily. Tactical brilliance is still often not matched by brilliance at the operational and strategic levels of military Art. We tend to get fixated on the existing force architectures and are often slow to innovate and change. The

Mahabharata set the military organizational paradigm that was to last till the 10th Century AD. This collapsed in the face of gunpowder, artillery and the Central Asian Cavalry that burst upon us from the Asian heartland.

From Warlords to Intelligence Czars

From a purely Attrition-oriented Paradigm, we see the radical transformation of the Indian Art of war at the hands of Kautilya. His brilliant and incisive analysis of the strengths and weaknesses of the Greek and Indian way of war was to lead him to the world's first revolution in Military Affairs. Kautilya, a Brahmin and an intellectual, envisioned the concept of information warfare. He built a state system whose prime resource was information. Through an army of spies he gathered information about every aspect of his own state and also of his neighboring and enemy states. Successive rings of spies and informers were used to keep a check on other spies and confirm the veracity and quality of their inputs. In a first wave agricultural civilization-building such a vast resource of information was an unparalleled intellectual feat with such primitive methods of documentation and record. The Brahmanical system relied upon a tremendous enhancement of human memorization abilities. The Brahmanical system laid major emphasis on prodigious feats of memory. The memorization and preservation of the oral tradition of the Vedas for instance set the stage for this first information revolution. The Mauryan State founded by Kautilya was based on information domination and the exploitation and manipulation of this information to shape the adversaries perception, responses and reactions. The Kautilian Paradigm went far beyond Alexander's Paradigm of military mobility. It took war to the psychological realm of the mind. It adopted the ultimate indirect approach in strategical terms. In war the aim was not the destruction of the enemy army or the enemy state. The prime target was the mind of the enemy commander and through him that of his troops in the field. The brilliant campaign was one that subdued the enemy without fighting. Sun Tzu comes to mind here,"For to win a thousand victories in a thousand battles is not the acme of excellence. Supreme excellence lies in subduing the enemy without fighting". To understand this major Paradigm shift in the Indian Art of War- we have only to contrast the Mahabharatan emphasis on attrition, chivalry and the direct force on force approach with the later sophistication of Kautilya's Paradigm of Information War and information dominance. The Mahabharata epic records the primal Indian military tradition of attrition. The Yadavas, the Shaubirs, the Dogritas and Tigritas, the Suryavanshis and Chandravanshi clans of Rajputs, the soldiers of Magadha and the Elephant warriors of Kamrupa and Naga warriors like Ghatotkacha, were all part of the Mahabharatan myth of chivalry and heroism. It was unchivalrous to strike down a wounded soldier or one stunned by war, or one fleeing the battlefield. Tactical brilliance and individual skill and prowess were highly prized. Tactical over sophistication however was not matched by skill at strategic or operational levels of military art or expertise in a more mobile style of war, as the Greeks were to wage many centuries later. However, when the Greek invasion came the Indian response was swift and astonishing.

Paradigmatic Changes and Challenges

The encounter of the Indian civilisation with the Greek civilisation provided a major civilisational challenge. In a typical stimulus-response chain, it forced the Indians to innovate and effect far-reaching changes in their ways of waging war. This Greek encounter exposed the attrition-oriented Indian armies of that era to the mobility-based paradigm of war that increased its pace and tempo far beyond anything that they had encountered earlier. The set piece battlefield (which was conceptualized in the chessboard and the game of chausar) gave way to encounter battles that could occur anywhere. The chariots were the first casualties of this more mobile form of war and the Elephants soon gained primacy in the Indian military organisation. However, at a deeper conceptual level- *Kautilyan intervention represents the onset of the Brahmanical (as opposed to the Kshatriya way of war that was enshrined in the Mahabharata)*. To counter a far superior mobility Paradigm- the Indian response went to levels of sophistication that were simply astonishing for that era .The Brahmanical approach to war led it beyond its physical dimensions to the realm of the mind- to information and psychological warfare to subversion, propaganda and disinformation operations of surprising sophistication. The most successful of these was exploiting the initial shock effect of war Elephants on the Greek Armies. This shock of encountering a new weapon system was woven skillfully into psychological-warfare themes that bit home unerringly; themes that exploited the war weariness and homesickness of the Greek troops and caused them to mutiny. This represents a paradigm shift from the Kshatriya way of war to the more mentalized Brahmanical art of war with its emphasis on the ultimate indirect approach- the sublimation of physical conflict to the psychological and informational domain of the mind.

To truly understand the magnitude of this Paradigm shift, we have first to understand the Mobility revolution in warfare unleashed by Alexander. Conflict was a largely localised and short-range affair before Alexander and his Greeks. It was confined to localised clashes and local wars between neighbouring city-states. For the first time in human history, Alexander raised a superbly trained Army that marched from Greece to Asia Minor, Iran, Central Asia and on to the Indo-Gangetic flood plains - fighting innumerable foes on the way and routing many rabble hosts of vast size (but little sophistication). The collision of the Greek and the Indic civilisation was a historic event. Alexander was check mated in India and his Greek tide rolled back. To counter the Greek Military Paradigm, the Indian essayed into the domain of Multidimensional warfare that combined the Military with the Non-Military aspects of war. This multidomain warfare made extensive use of Information and Psychological warfare to weaken and unbalance the enemy. It was a truly astonishing intellectual feat for that ancient era. Such theories have again resurfaced after the Gulf War of 1991.

The Clash of Civilisations

The clash of the two civilisations had a decisive impact on the history of the region. It caused a significant churning in the Indian civilisation. The great Indian Grand Master of war and politics, the famous Kautilya (or Chanakya) pondered deeply over the lessons of this civilisational conflict. He realised that the more mobile Greek Military Paradigm had taken war to a different league altogether. Analysing the structure of the ancient Indic Armies he realised that their over-reliance on the chariots as a mobility and command and control platform had been their undoing. He was equally quick to realise that the Elephant was a far better military platform (both for mobility and for command and control). He was equally quick to realise the tremendous shock impact of the employment of elephants in mass. He exploited this psychological shock effect to the hilt through a brilliant information warfare campaign that halted the world conquering Greek Army in its tracks literally.

Information Dominance in a First Wave Army

The critical aspect is that within the space of a few years, the Indian civilisation had unleashed a magnificent response to the Greek invasion and military challenge. Thus, Alexander began his invasion in 327 BC. In just 3 years, he was back at Surru in Persia (324 BC) Chandragupta (the protege of Kautilya) had consolidated his hold upon the State of Magadha in 320 BC. He took just 15 years to transform India from a civilisational to a political entity. In 305 BC Chandragupta had inflicted a humiliating defeat on the Greek Satrap Selukos Niketor and consolidated the Frontier regions and invasion routes via Afghanistan. Greek sophistry on the battlefield had been countered by resort to an even higher level of sophistication in warfare. It marked a cardinal turning point in the ancient Indian Art of War. Conflict was raised to its ultimate dimension of the mind, where battles are ultimately lost or won. This, in historic terms, represents the birth of Information Warfare in an ancient First Wave or Agricultural civilisational setting. The computer revolution was still almost three millenniums away. What this ancient information revolution relied upon was the excellent Brahmanical resource of human memory banks. Generations of Brahmins had been taught to memorize by rote hundreds of thousands of verses of sacred texts and pass on the oral tradition from generation to generation. Kautilya utilized this excellent brahmanical human resource to generate an information revolution. Peter Rosen has made uncharitable remarks in his book (India and its Armies) that seems to suggest that Indians had a penchant for "treachery". The Indian people are intrinsically fond of drama or *'Abhinaya'* (role-playing). Hence Kautilya was able to raise an army of spies, informers and sources. They were so numerous in number that Megasthenes felt they belonged to a separate caste as such. They formed the basis of the primitive information warfare revolution generated by Kautilya in the millennium before the birth of Christ. In effect this saw the employment of human Bio-Computers that still remain superior to any silicon-based computer. *The transition from the Mahabharatan Paradigm of war to the Kautilyan Paradigm marks the transition from a Kshatriya to a Brahmanical tradition of war in Ancient India. It represents a Paradigm Shift in the art of war from the physical to a psychological plane.* The Greeks had graduated from attrition to mobility. Military Mobility has a shock effect on the mind of a slower and more sluggish opponent. Alexander won all his famous victories on the strength of this transformation in the way of war. The Greek Army was a closed micro society of professionals for whom war had become a way of life. Alexander is hailed today as one of the Great Captains of wars who enunciated the Mobility Paradigm and the basic Arabella (penetration) and "Single Canne" (or single Envelopment) manoeuvre. The world is yet to recognize the true outcome of his contest with the Indian civilization. Kautilya halted Alexander's advance by taking war to even subtler dimensions of the mind. He used information warfare and psychological warfare to exploit the Greek soldiers war weariness and the tremendous shock effect of encountering Indian War Elephants. He used the psychological tools of rumor, exaggeration and embellishment to weave lurid themes of Indian Armies with literally thousands of monstrous war Elephants trampling down the Greeks in a virtual avalanche. The writings of some ancient Greek historians of that period have graphically described the impact of the Indian war-elephants; on how they terrified the horses, how they trampled the soldiers underfoot, how they gored them with their tusks and above all, how they entwined the soldiers in their trunks, dashed them to the ground with such terrific force that it split open their armour and smashed their bones and skulls. Kautilya's spies embellished such gory tales and spread rumors of thousands upon thousands of such war-elephants with the Nanda armies. This psy-war campaign was enough to halt a world conquering Greek Army in its tracks. Not only was the Greek Army halted, it mutinied, and all of Alexander's oratory, was not sufficient to rouse his demoralized troops. Alexander was forced to retreat.

Supreme excellence lies in subduing the enemy without fighting!

Not only did Kautilya prove to be a Master of Information Warfare, he proved equally adept in analyzing the physical dimensions of war. He realized that the Indian Force structure had placed too heavy a reliance on the chariots. These lacked cross-country mobility and were therefore not suited as spear-heads for attack or command and control platforms in more mobile operations. He effected the significant shift from Chariots to War Elephants. The shock effect of the employment in mass of these war elephants had been well-established. What was even more significant was their cross-country mobility in all kinds of terrain (less deserts). They were excellent for river crossing, for attacking forts and battering down gates and walls. They were superb command and control and fighting platforms. Kautilya made elephants the pride of his army and the basis of the mobility revolution that he was to unleash subsequently. Kautilya increased the number of war-elephants in the Imperial Mauryan Army from 3000 to 9000. Within a space of a few decades, not only had Kautilya halted and turned back the conquering Greek armies of Alexander, he had consolidated the Mauryan Empire, effected a political unification of the Indian civilisational entity and secured its frontier up till Afghanistan. He had led his ruler Chandra Gupta to attack the Greek Satrap Selukos Niketor. Selukos was decisively defeated and had to secede the provinces of Baluchistan and Afghanistan and also give his daughter in marriage to Chandragupta.

So much for Greek Conquest!

From Psychological to Ideological Warfare

The transition from the Mahabharatan to the Kautilyan Paradigm of war in ancient India represents the transition from the Kshatriya to the Brahmanical tradition of war. War was increasingly shifted to its psychological or informational domain. This process reached its ultimate logical conclusion with the subsequent rise of Emperor Ashoka — the greatest Indian monarch of all times. Ashoka turned from Dig Vijay or physical conquest to ideological conquest, to a conquest of hearts and minds. *He sublimated war from a clash of blood and steel to a clash of ideas and ideologies.* He spread the Buddhist ideology to all corners of Asia. Ashoka's reign saw the Indian civilisation at its pinnacle of glory and achievement. In a first wave agricultural world, an army of Indian Buddhist monks carried out an ideological conquest of almost the whole of Asia (to include Tibet, Bhutan, Sri Lanka, Myanmar, China, Korea, Japan, Central Asia, Mongolia and the whole of South East Asia). World history has no other parallel of an ideological campaign and conquest of this magnitude. This Indian ideological empire has survived to this day and age. It has lasted almost 2500 years and outlived all empires based on physical conquest by the sword and torch of pillaging armies. It was a conquest of the mind that has no parallels in human history. Sadly for India, the Kautilyan tradition did not last long. The original Indian military school of war of the Mahabharatan age resurfaced, subsequently. It is premised on attrition, direct force on force engagements and chivalry. It represents the innate disposition of the Indian soldiery and military leadership. It is the paradigm to which we gravitate time and again because it suits our basic genius and temperament. It is the original Indian way of war. It is enshrined in our folklore, ballads and legends; in the war songs that are sung around campfires. It is premised on heroism as an end in itself. This Kshatriya way of war has resurfaced time and again, and reasserted its historic validity in the Indian context. Stratagems and deception are abhorrent to this pristine way of war. It is premised on chivalry, honor and glory. It is our strength. It has also time and again, been our undoing, especially when we have been faced with cruel and unscrupulous enemies who had exploited all that is good in the Indian psyche to our infinite sorrow. The Mahabharatan epic therefore enshrines the basal and original Indian tradition of war. It is more central and endemic to the Indian civilisational context than the later sophistry of Kautilya. *The Mahabharata represents the Kshatriya tradition of war as opposed to the Brahmanical tradition of Kautilya*. The Mahabharata laid emphasis on bravery and gallantry in pure force on force engagements that relied entirely on attrition to wear down their enemies. Kautilya raised the Indian civilisation to its pinnacle of glory. But Kautilya forms a brief interlude of brilliance that flowered in the world's first information warfare campaign. These blossomed later into the ideological conquest of all Asia by the Indian ideology of Buddhism. War had been sublimated not just to the plane of the mind but to a far higher dimension of the spirit. Today the world has become a global village. The Hedonist ideology of consumerism has been propagated across the continents and seas. It is a borderless world where frontiers have become irrelevant. All this has been achieved with the help of the information revolution; with satellites and television. The ancient Indian civilisation achieved all this and more without the paraphernalia of information technology. It was accomplished by an army of Buddhist monks dedicated to the spread of an altruistic and universal ideology. The consumerist culture is based upon selfishness. The Buddhist ideology was based on compassion and altruism. Hence the ease with which it spread. That was our acme of achievement. It was also in one way our undoing. Centuries of the sway of a pacifist ideology led to a steep decline in matters military. The art of war atrophied. Armies went to seed. The traditions of Kautilya were forgotten. With the disintegration of the Mauryan Empire, the Indian civilisation lost its political unity and military cohesion; centrifugal tendencies came to the fore again and led to our decline.

The Clash of Civilizations: The Indo-Greek Encounter,

Alexander's invasion therefore represents a classic clash of civilizations. The Greek military machine had been perfected over almost two decades of inter city-state warfare in Greece. In these years a highly professional and well-trained Greek Army emerged. In terms of strategic mobility and tactical brilliance, it was far ahead of its times and launched a brilliant campaign that was unheard of in its range and sweep. From Greece it poured out into Asia Minor, Iran, Central Asia, Afghanistan and into the Indo-Gangetic Plains. This Greek invasion (though it touched only the fringes of the Indian civilization) came as a great cultural shock. The civilisational challenge of the Greeks led to great inner ferment in the Indian Civilization. The shock of the impact of the Greeks led to the first Indian political consolidation. From a civilizational entity — the shock of the Greek encounter forced it to transform itself into a political entity and led to Nation State Formation in terms of the rise of the Mauryan Empire.

The Political Impact

In the Early Vedic Age (2000 to 1000 BC) political organisations in India were largely tribal and consisted of kings and chieftains guided by tribal councils called Samitis and Sabhas. The early Vedic Aryans were nomadic and pastoral. With their horses and chariots they destroyed the far more sophisticated urban civilisations of the Indus and Saraswati river vallies and caused a civilisational regression to an earlier stage of political evolution. As the Vedic Aryans expanded beyond the Indus-Punjab tracts into the Indo-Gangetic Plains, they transited to agriculture. This led to their permanent settlements and the rise of fixed territorial units or Janapadas (or small states.) Most of these states were monarchial but there were a significant number administered on Republican and Democratic lines. By the later Vedic Age (1000 BC to 600 BC) the political map of Ancient India had evolved into 16 Maha Janapadas or large territorial states (and a number of smaller Janapadas). These 16 Maha Janapadas were Gandhara, Kamboja, Assaka, Vatsa, Avanti, Shursena, Chedi, Malla, Kuru, Panchala, Matsya, Vrijji, Anga, Kashi, Koshala and Magadha. The Mahabharata War occurred in the second Vedic Age and possibly led to the rise of the Republican clans over the hereditary monarchies of the era. Initially Kashi was the most important politico-economic center as it was the leading area of textile manufacturing and learning. Slowly Magadha gained more importance and by the time of Alexanders invasion, the Nandas of Magadha were the main Indian military power. What Alexander encountered were the outlying and peripheral micro-states that did not really qualify as Maha Janapadas. However the invasion was not by some barbarian hordes but a highly sophisticated and well-organised civilisation of matching scale and antiquity. It is relevant to note *that the idea of Rashtra or Nation had emerged in the later Vedic period in Ancient India*. A number of verses, especially in the later *Atharva Veda*, mention the word "Rashtra" and express patriotic sentiments based not just on a civilisational unity but on a territorial centric nation-state as it were. This Brahmanical idea of a national (as opposed to a civilisational unity) was therefore prevalent long before the invasion of Alexander. It is usually however the idea of the "non-self" which strengthens the idea of "Self". The Greek civilisational challenge for the first time made the Indian scholars and political thinkers like Kautilya, painfully aware of the perils of the lack of political unity. Ancient India was fragmented and splintered into a mosaic of Maha Janapadas and minor Janapadas that were constantly feuding with one another. The rivalry of Ambhi of Taxshila and Puru of the Cis Jhelum-Ravi tracts proved fatal in the initial encounters with Alexander. In this period of a civilisational peril, Chanakya realised the need for national unity and a civilisational response. His appeals to the Nandas of Magadha (then the prime military power in India) fell on deaf ears. To the contrary, legend has it that Chanakya (Kautilya) was insulted and thrown out of the Nanda Court for his pains. This was a profound depth experience that shook Kautilya to his psychological core. He went forward to stall the Greek advance. Lacking the military backing of the Nanda Army, he relied instead upon a very skillful psychological and information warfare campaign. Once the Greek invaders were halted and forced to retreat- he turned his attention to forging the National unity that had already been talked of as "Rashtra" in the later Vedas. In consolidating the imperial Mauryan State Kautilya transformed India's civilisational unity into a political unification. This however could not have been done in the absence of the Greek civilisational challenge. It was the threat of the Greek "non-self", the "other", that helped to crystallise the Indian sense of "self" or nation-hood. The Imperial Mauryan State that Chanakya helped to establish was a vast and highly centralized state. It controlled almost every aspect of economic activity in the Indian sub-continent. Hermann Kulke and Deitmar Rothermund feel that the rise of Magadha was due to the following factors :

- It controlled the regions for mining Iron ore.
- It controlled the ancient trade routes.
- It had an assured supply of war elephants from the Eastern Forest Tracts of Assam and other North-Eastern States. Iron Technology and war elephant were the basis of its military power.

It opened up vast new tracts of lands for agriculture— so that a considerable surplus could be generated. It controlled trade, manufacture and mining. The State owned collective farms, ran eating homes and gambling/liquor bars (which were prime centers for gathering of information and intelligence) and taxed all economic activity in the state. From these vast revenues, it raised a ponderous, standing professional Army of 650,000 - a remarkable feat for that day and age. It also raised and maintained a vast and elaborate bureaucracy and an information and intelligence network of unparalleled sophistication. Human intelligence was its prime agency *and it raised a vast army of spies and informants to help it gain information dominance (both internally and externally)*. The most critical aspect is that the Imperial Mauryan State disarmed and pacified the countryside and to that extent laid the basis for the classical trinity of the State, the unarmed population and the professional Armed Forces (that form a distinct micro-society). Thus, in the earlier Mahabharata period, we see coalition warfare between a series of Maha Janapadas that were arrayed against each other in a Civil War of Armageddon proportions. By the time of Kautilya we see the transformation of India's civilisational unity to political unification and the formation of a highly sophisticated and centralised nation-state in place of a mosaic of feuding Janapadas.

Military Changes. These have already been recounted earlier in great detail and only need to be summed up here: -

(a) The prevailing Military Paradigm in Ancient India at the time of Alexander's invasion was that of the Mahabharata. It was an attrition-oriented Paradigm that relied on pure force on force engagements in set piece battlefields. The Armies were elaborate structures of four arms (Chariots, Elephants, Cavalry and Infantry) primed for tactical level combat aimed at annihilation of the enemy in set piece battles.

(b) Alexander had introduced a far more mobile form of war. He had led a strategic campaign of conquest from Europe (Greece) across Asia to the Indian Subcontinent. The Greeks outmanouvered the Indian armies primed for set piece battles of attrition.

(c) In his initial campaign of 327 BC Alexander advanced into the Punjab. Later his troops mutinied and he had to fight his way out along the Indus River course to the Sea.

(d) Thus no major military contest developed between the main Indian Military Power of that era - the Nandas and Alexander's Greek Army.

(e) However, as Alexander fought his way out he was opposed primarily by the Tribal Republican clans of the North West. They fought him individually. No civilisational coalition was organized to oppose Alexander. His campaign led to a virtual decimation of the numerous Tribal Republics of North Western India (which had come to the fore after the Mahabharatan epic war). This laid the way for the consolidation of monarchial rule in ancient India.

(f) The Maha janapada of Magadha had attained military pre-eminence in ancient India much before the advent of Alexander. Ajatashatru had expanded the power of Magadha. His successors, the Nandas had made Magadha the most powerful Maha janapada in the Indian Geo-political landscape. The Nandas are reputed to have maintained a standing Army of 200,000 Infantry, 20,000 Cavalry, 2000 chariots and 3000 elephants (Dr DN Jha, Ancient India in Historical Outline). The Nandas however refused to do their civilisational duty and contest Alexander. Kautilya who later installed his protege Chandragupta on the throne of Magadha overthrew them.

(g) The consolidation of the Imperial Mauryan Empire, for the first time transformed Indian civilisational unity into political unity and led to the clear cut establishment of a historic nation state that was highly centralised and very well administered.

(h) Militarily, the Mauryans now emulated the Greek Mobility Paradigm. The Chariots were found unfit for mobile warfare and long cross country movement. These were phased out and the elephants became the prime shock Arm. War elephants were employed in Mass.The number of war elephants was raised from 3000 to 9000.

(i) The Greek example led to the establishment of huge, standing and professional Army and Navy that were competently managed by a board of officers in the Imperial Mauryan dispensation.

(j) Information dominance and covert operations were the prime instruments of Kautilyan warfare. No conventional military operations were launched without a prolonged campaign to destabilise, weaken and unbalance an opponent. Conventional military operations were usually a coup de main operation that exploited and mopped up in the wake of the Covert War (or Kuta Yudha) campaign.

(k) The Imperial Mauryan Empire relied upon a very scientific consolidation of its frontiers and went in for a forward defence of the realm in Afghanistan and Baluchistan.

(l) It launched a proactive offensive defense by attacking the Greek Satrap Selukos Niketaor and driving him out of the Indian border regions.

(m) *Internally the Imperial Mauryan Army pacified and disarmed the country side, thus paving the way for the establishment of a proper Nation State with the Trinitarian structure of the state, its armed forces and the unarmed people.* This gave the State a monopoly of violence and power. "The Rashatra" of the later Vedic hymns had become a geo political reality with the advent of the Mauryan Empire.

Thus from the Mahabharata period to the Mauryan age, we see the transformation of India from a civilisational entity that was fragmented into a number of feuding states to a political entity that was highly centralized and became a proper nation state in the West phalian sense of the word (Nation states came into being in Europe with the treaty of Westphalia in 1648). Such a nation state could only come into being once the political authority had disarmed and pacified the populace and acquired a monopoly of violence. In military terms, the art of war transited from the force on force, attrition paradigm to a highly sophisticated Mauryan form, which laid great emphasis on prolonged covert action campaigns to destabilize and weaken opposing states before launching any conventional military operations. The Mauryan State therefore laid great emphasis on information dominance, information war, psy-war and covert action. Conventional war thus became a last resort option and an instrument for delivering the final coup de grace after elaborate and extended campaigns of destabilization that destroyed the politico-military balance of the target nation.

The Indian Period of Warring States

Chinese military theories crystallised in the so-called period of the Warring States (450-300 BC). A large number of military theorists went pedalling their military theories to the Chinese kings and Dukes of the six major states of China (Ch'i, Ch'u, Ch'in, Wei, Han and Chao). One of the most famous of them was Sun Tzu (Sun Zi). These incessant wars lasted for a 150 years and gave full scope to the military theorists to test their theories in actual combat. These 150 years of conflict saw the flowering of the Chinese military genius to the its fullest form.

There is a school of thought that Kautilyas Arthashastra was not written in the brief period preceding Alexanders invasion. It was a far older text that had been compiled in the Indian period of the warring kingdom — the period of the earlier Vedic age that saw the rise of the sixteen Mahajanapadas and incessant fighting and combat and competition between them. The theory of the Mandala of states could only have emerged from such a crucible of conflict that entailed many states and dealt with supra national alliances and engineering of blocs of states. This ancient text was capitalized by Chankya who put it to use to defeat all the other Mahajanapadas, and forged a single United Indian Civilisatioal State under the imperial banner of Magadha.

What must however be emphasised in conclusion however, is the fact that the Kautilyan interlude was only a brief episode of strategic brilliance that lasted at best for a century of far reaching effects. It was followed by a gradual regression to the primal attrition paradigm of the Mahabharata, which remains the basic Indian art of war.

10

Administration and Training

ADMINISTRATION

The Mahabharata epic mentions that an elaborate logistical infrastructure existed to keep the combatants supplied with the wherewithal to fight. The armies had concentrated in vast camps with rows upon rows of tents. The following categories of non-combatants accompanied the armies :

(a) Load carriers.
(b) Food suppliers
(c) Doctors with medical outfits.
(d) Veterinary surgeons for horses and elephants.
(e) Field workshops for repair and limited manufacture of weapons.
(f) Priests, bards and war musicians.
(g) Entertainers - including dancing girls and prostitutes.
(h) Field treasuries for disbursement of pay and allowances and cash grants and rewards.

The non-combatants were generally spared in war by the enemy. All this constituted a monstrous 'tail'. However the teeth-to-tail ratio of the Indian armies in various periods has continued to be lopsided. They reached fairly outlandish proportions in the Moghul period when entire harems and mobile courts were transferred to the theatre of operations. This severely curtailed mobility. This drag on mobility was shed by Shivaji, who relied primarily upon the cavalry. There were no women in his camps which were kept to a spartan minimum in terms of luxury and comfort. The troops generally lived off the land. The present Indian Army also had to shed a lot of 'tail' in the wake of the 1962 debacle.

Pay and Accounts

The soldiers of both armies wore distinctive insignias and received regular pay and allowances including grants for acts of bravery. This indicates a regular standing army. However, just before the battle conscription appears to have been resorted to swell the ranks and achieve peak mobilization. The soldiers wore armour of leather hides. The commanders wore distinctive armour — sometimes said to be made of gold and studded with precious jewels — complete with helmets with plumes and gorgeous standards.

Fighting (F) Echelons

Long rows of carts carrying arrows and spare weapons and food and water provisions accompanied the chariots into battle and served as modern F Echelons or the A1 and A2 Echelons.

TRAINING

Military training was taken very seriously in the Mahabharata. Guidelines are laid in the *Shanti Parva* for the selection of soldiers. Their qualitative requirements are listed out in fair detail (should be tall, slim, tough and quick in movement; also be expert in climbing, riding, drill and fencing, and fighting in various *Vyuhas* or formations). Stress was laid upon building a military character so that soldiers would remain calm and firm in victory and defeat. It is a very interesting fact that the Indian Military Academy situated at Dehradun is the present West Point of the Indian Army. The word 'Dehradun' is a derivative of the historical 'Dera-Drona' which means Camp of Drona. It is most interesting to note that the present Indian Military Academy is situated exactly where Dronacharya had established his school to train the Pandava and Kaurava princes some 2500 years ago!

Dronacharya's war academy was headed by the great sage himself, with Kripacharya as the second-in-command. The academy had the following major sections :

(a) *The Archery Cell.* Headed by Dronacharya himself.
(b) *Royal School of Conduct.* Headed by the great theorist, Sanjay.
(c) *Philosophy.* Vedas and meditation were taught by the great sage Martandya and the royal priests. Ved Vyasa was some kind of an emeritus professor here.

(d) *Mace Training Cell.* Headed by Balarama, the elder brother of Krishna.
(e) *Physical Proficiency School.* Taught boxing, wrestling and javelin and shakti throwing.
(f) *School of Animal Training.* Taught horse and elephant management in battle.
(g) *School of Fine Arts.* Music, dance and instrumental music.

Specialist Training

There were specialist *acharyas* (teachers) for training in various branches of war, e.g. Dronacharya, Kripacharya, Parashurama and Balarama. Leaders and princes were trained intensively in individual and collective combat — especially the theory and practice of various *Vyuhas*. Training started in early childhood and went on till the age of 25 for the royal gentry.

Animal Trainers

There were specialist and highly qualified animal trainers for the war mounts :

(a) *Gaja-dhyaksha* was the trainer of elephants. To handle them he had to be a man of a calm and stable temperament and lofty character.
(b) *Ashwa-dhyaksha* was the trainer of horses. Krishna, incidentally, was said to be a great trainer of war animals (horses, elephants, etc.). He had a very uncanny ability to empathize with these creatures and understood them well. His very presence is said to have a calming influence upon war mounts.

Espionage

Espionage and the continuous acquisition of intelligence was a very vital function of state craft. Elaborate instructions for the recruitment, training and employment of spies are given by Bhishma to Yudhisthira in the *Shanti Parva*. The intelligence-gathering and state security functions seemed to overlap. Basically agents employed were of two types :

(a) *Legals.* Diplomats, ambassadors and emissaries who operated under legal cover.
(b) *Illegals.* Traders, wandering monks, dispossessed agriculturists,

people who nurse a grievance against the enemy king, dancing girls or prostitutes, old maids or wandering nuns and a class of people called Teekha (professionals at administering poison) were used to operate without legal cover.

The multiplicity of sources is stressed upon. There were many concentric espionage rings. Agents must be deputed to keep watch over other agents and cross check the veracity and quality of their inputs.

Security

The *Manu Smriti* says that the king should trust no one and keep even his own queen under continuous surveillance. All relatives, ministers and important courtiers must similarly be watched. Excellent espionage and security networks existed in the time of the *Mahabharata*.

11

Mahabharata's Relevance to Present Conditions

Is the *Mahabharata* just an archaic myth that has no relevance to our times? Is it at best just a record of a very primitive war fought with bows and arrows and swords and lances? What relevance does its study have to the modern battlefield that teems with tanks with integrated fire control system and Chobham armour and precision guided munitions (PGMs), armed helicopters and nuclear weaponry?

The answer is, if Sun Tzu's *The Art of War,* which represents a similar (in fact inferior) state of development of weapons technology, can inspire a Liddell Hart in this century or a Guderian or Manstein, what prevents us from seeking inspiration from the Mahabharata?

We need to look at the *Mahabharata* not just for emotional reasons of national pride but because it has a lot to offer. The weapon systems and technologies change — the basic manoeuvres and strategies of war seem to remain constant. A 'Canne' or 'Double Canne' or an 'Arabella Manoeuvre' is still as relevant to armoured forces as it was to Alexander's or, Hannibal's cavalry.

Let us isolate from this study some of the commonalities and relevant factors :

(a) *Short-duration, high-intensity conflicts.* The Mahabharata War lasted only 18 days. At these levels its intensity was very high. All our post-Independence conflicts have been under a month in duration (1965 - 22 days' war, 1971 - 14 days' war etc.)

(b) *Campaign season in the subcontinent.* The *Mahabharata* mentions the

period from November to March (months of Aghayana to Chaitra). A brief survey will indicate that *all* our post independence wars have indeed taken place in this period e.g. :

- 1962 Sino-Indian War — November-December 1962
- 1965 Indo-Pak War — September-October 1965
- 1971 Bangladesh War — November-December 1971

(c) *Mass regular armies.* At over 12 lakhs the Indian Army today is the fourth largest army in the world. This is in keeping with traditions as they came down from the *Mahabharata* era and the Mauryan period.

(d) *Penchant for Bhishma's direct approach.* As mentioned earlier, there were two military schools of thought :

- *The traditional* one based upon the direct approach — as propagated by the *Dhanurveda* and Bhishma.
- *The indirect Kuta Yudha* approach of Krishna and Ashwathama. It is highly interesting to note that the Bhishma School of War still has a predominant influence over the Indian military mind. Note the following facts.

(e) *War must be fought between equals.* The *Mahabharata* is the source of not only all that is noble and good in the Indian military tradition but also of that which is its bane — its chivalry and its abject failure to adopt the indirect approach in strategy. This has proved very costly in the subsequent phases of Indian history. However, a study of the *Mahabharata* shows that these heroic attitudes are deeply ingrained and will take a major effort to shed. In all our post-Independence wars, our armoured divisions were used only against enemy armour — in a plain tank killer role. It seems 'unfair' to us to use them against the enemy's infantry or unprotected areas. Various tactical arguments are forwarded to explain this use (rather-non-use) of our armoured formations. It is a part of our inheritance which stated that chariots must only attack chariots. The sooner we get rid of this chivalrous and 'sporting' approach the better it will be for us. War is not a sport to be played at the exchequer's expense. It is a ruthless continuation of state policy — by other means. And the other means are meant to be violent and purposive. From an armed force the size of ours, a country has the right to expect victories of the Bangladesh order, not stalemates of the 1965 pattern.

(*f*) *Abhorrence of covert and intelligence operations*. Kuta Yudha methods were despised by 'honourable' Indian soldiers of the *Mahabharata* period. The tragedy is that even today our Indian regular soldiers still tend to despise these methods as unethical or unsoldierly. Notice the fact that officers of our intelligence corps have no bright career opportunities *vis-a-vis* the other arms. It appears intelligence and covert operations are second-rate side shows for which only second-grade officers can or need be spared. This attitutde has been further reinforced by our British military heritage.

(*g*) *All-arms team concept*. There were four basic arms in the *Mahabharata* period. The excellent balance of these at all unit and formation levels indicates a clear grasp of the all-arms team concept. The aim would be to have a homogeneous army. At present, all modern armies have been making efforts in this direction albeit with tanks and mechanized infantry.

(*h*) *Triangular Organizational Pattern*. This seems to have inadvertently come down to us from the *Mahabharata* period.

(*i*) *Aprakshya Yudha* or *Covert Operations*. In recent times there has been an exploison of interest in low-intensity conflict and special forces. Indians have also begun to pay some attention to the covert action aspect of military operations.

(*j*) *Psychological Warfare*. The grand masters of the *Mahabharata* were experts at psychological warfare. Their main aim was at all times the mind of the enemy commander. Indian operations in Bangladesh showed a remarkable grasp of this aspect of psychological warfare.

(*k*) *Dharma Yudha* or *'Just War Concept'*. A war should be 'just' in terms of cause or motive. If the end or cause is just, any means — ethical or otherwise — may be used in its prosecution. Our war in Bangladesh admirably fits the *Dharma Yudha* concept.

Lessons to be Learnt

We have learned the *Mahabharata* war at length from its conceptual aspect. We have compared the state of the art obtaining then to the Sun Tzu period of Chinese military development, and found it comparable if not superior in many aspects. We have also listed the factors and concepts that still hold relevance for our modern Indian Army in the pursuance of its wars on the

Indian subcontinent. What are the lessons that we can usefully learn from this magnum opus on the ancient Indian school of war? These could be :

(a) *Dharma Yudha - Just War.* The Indian Armed Forces have always been used in the past for the prosecution of wars that have been just in the cause analysis aspect. The most outstanding example is India's liberation of the persecuted millions of Sonar Bangladesh. We should ensure that from the 'Dharma' aspect our wars are just. If the cause is just, no inhibitions must come in the way of employing any means, howsoever foul or unethical for a ruthless drive for total victory.

(b) *Psychological warfare.* War must be aimed at the mind of the enemy commander. A good battle is not judged by the number of corpses left on the battlefield but by the results it achieves. The casualties in the Bangladesh theatre of operations in 1971 were far less than in the Western theatre. That does not imply that the troops fought better in the Western sector. In fact compared to the brilliant blitzkrieg in the East our campaign in the West appears lack-lustre (we must keep in mind the overall war aims though). In the East the war was directly aimed at the minds of the enemy commanders. Thus, though large bodies of the Pakistani troops were left intact their will to fight collapsed. That is the acme of skill. This was made possible by the use of the indirect approach and the expanding torrent concept.

(c) *Adoption of Vyuha methodology.* The use of battle drills in fluid mechanized operations, especially the well-tried 'T-formation' (Shakta Vyuha) that has been used with such success by the Germans in North Africa, is most essential. In adopting this methodology we will be followng a way of war that suits the genius of our people. Vyuhas were battle arrays and battle drills for coordinating the actions of four different speed manoeuvre masses on the battlefield (the manoeuvre masses of the chariots, the elephants, the horsed cavalry and the infantry). In practical terms there is much to learn from the theory and practise of Vyuhas for our modern mechanised operations.

(d) *Covert operations - Aprakshya Yudha* to weaken and destabilize potential enemies. This 'silent war' should be continuous process. The conflict spectrum is a continuum. Today the distinction between war and peace has become highly blurred and indistinct. An alert conflict manager must at all times seek to instigate rebellions and terrorist movements in an enemy state. This will serve to destroy its politico-military balance and help an attacker to overthrow it with ease in a regular war. Covert operations must precede and prepare the way for a regular conventional attack.

(e) *Improving our all-arms integration.* At present we have achieved this at best down to the combat group level. We must lay more stress on all arms integration at the grassroots (combat team) level by making such groupings *permanent,* based upon predictable theatre requirements. In doing this we will be taking a leaf straight out of the *Mahabharata*.

12

Racial Motifs of War : The Indian Inheritance

AN ETHICAL BASIS OF WAR

Modern statecraft is based on the ruthless and cold-blooded pursuit of national interests. Even Kautilya's *Arthashastra* is eloquent upon this aspect. Morality and ethical standards seem to have little relevance today in the rarefied dimension of international relations. What is true at the level of interpersonal relations does not seem to hold true at the level of interaction between nations.

The *Mahabharata* epic however seems to lay a great deal of stress on 'Dharma' as the basis of warfighting. *Dharma* here does not denote religion. Rather it denotes eternal and abiding principles of justice and morality that have a universal and timeless character. To that extent a 'Dharma Yudha' is not the same as a Jehad or a crusade. The *Mahabharata* was not fought between the adherents of different faiths or religions. It was a major civil war, the memory of which is enshrined in this epic. In the racial myth it is a landmark, an Armageddon which is said to have exhausted the Indian civilization and led to its decline.

This war took a long time to brew. Many sincere attempts were made to stave it off by diplomatic initiatives and peace overtures. Munich however failed to prevent the Second World War. So also all these peace initiatives seem to have failed to prevent this apocalypse. However, the long build-up to the war highlighted three aspects. Let us study these in detail.

War : Last Resort Option

The Indians viewed war as the last resort option not to be undertaken lightly. However, in the end, war remained a Clausewitzian last resort — a continuation of state policy by 'other means'. War is clearly viewed as a last resort policy option in this epic. This war is 'total' in many aspects inasmuch as the total mobilization of the state's war-making potential is involved.

However, in the epic a whole set of curious limitations have been put to control collateral damage to civilian population and targets. Territorial or political objectives have little relevance in this war. Campaigns are not launched over a wide front. Rather armies concentrate on a given battlefield for a direct contest — a head-on collision in the form of a grand tournament. Today, we can smile indulgently at such a primitive view of war. However, most of the anicent battles in Indian military history followed this pattern. The lack of means of communications to control battles dispersed over a wide geographical area dictated this form of combat.

The Kurukshetra battlefield somehow has emerged as a historical battle area that has witnessed repeated, decisive military contests (Panipat is merely an extension of Kurukshetra). Possibly the political centre of gravity of ancient India was based on two centres - the Hastinapur-Delhi region and Patliputra in Magadha (that conforms to the Bengal-Bihar region). Political power in ancient India oscillated between these two poles. A forward defence of the Northern centre of gravity (Delhi) called for a battle area somewhere around Kurukshetra or Panipat. That is where the most decisive battles of Indian military history have repeatedly been fought. This concept of warfighting is primitive and is dictated by the constraints of communication technologies and means of military mobility.

However, the Mongols under Ghengiz Khan and Sabutai had overcome this limited paradigm and actualized the expanding torrent concept of attack with horse-based armies itself. This technique was subsequently picked up by Liddell Hart, and practised by the Germans and the Israelis with tanks. The Indian military tradition remained fixated on the single battle where all was won or lost in a single battlefield. Today when we smile indulgently at such primitive views of war we fail to recognize that we have not outgrown this peculiar Indian mindset till this day.

The *Mahabharata* not only highlights our military strengths but also pinpoints the fatal and endemic flaws in our military make-up which we need to guard against. Even today, Indian armour enthusiasts regard the tank as the best anti-tank weapon, and this becomes the basis for the commitment of our mechanized formations in battle. This brings us right back to the *Mahabharata* paradigm — chariots must attack chariots, elephants must engage elephants. We must outgrow this fixation.

The Germans used tanks in preference against soft-skinned infantry to effect deep and strategic penetrations. German operational art emphasized break-out to the depth to destroy the enemy gun areas and headquarters. Soviet military philosophy also did not regard the tank as a purely anti-tank weapon system. That task is left to specialized anti-tank units and tank formations were used instead as instruments of shock and deep penetration. The ancient Indian employment of elephants as shock troops has had mixed results in Indian history.

The psychological impact of a mass of war elephants can be staggering but in actual practice this led to mixed results. Stricken elephants were indiscriminate in their rampage. This placid animal did not lend itself well to controlled employment in combat situations due to the weakness of its protective hide and its vulnerable spots. The horse has proved a better war mount in battle. The elephant had replaced the chariot as the prime shock aim. However once gun powder came on the battlefield the days of the elephant were numbered.

Correcting military overcaution : Cultivating the gambler's instinct

The slide to war is tinged with political overcaution. A slow built-up is called for. Attitudes and opinions are orchestrated gradually. Public opinion is driven to the point of outrage. It demands action. However, once the political decision is taken the military response should be dramatic. Long lead times give adequate time for build-up and preparation. Such a cautions political approach gave military success to the Pandavas. Duryodhana was impulsive and hotheaded. He impetuously plunged into conflict time and again. Fools rush in where angels fear to tread. Many times Duryodhana landed himself into impossible situations/humiliations because he rushed in blindly and had to be rescued by his hated cousins whom he despised. Karna is an other extreme. He is a warrior and loves war for the sake of war itself. He is thirsting for a mighty war that can pitch him against mighty rivals so that he can establish his supremacy as the world's greatest archer. His whole life is a quest for combat.

Risk taking

The political overcaution is however contrasted with a military tradition that deliberately fosters the gambler's instinct. The military leader is advised to cultivate this habit of risk taking. Like a gambler he must learn to pitch everything at the throw of a dice as it were. An Israeli commandment for young officers says 'Attack! Attack! Attack'. The second commandment amplifies 'In the attack Risk! Risk! Risk'. The Kshatriya in the epic period was tradition-bound not to turn down a challenge to gamble. The aim was not to inculcate gambling as a virtue but to inculcate the 'gambler's orientation' in the military commander. It was to instil in him the risk-taking orientation — the mindset to grasp an opportunity and pitch everything in one single turn of the dice. The crucial decision comes from such an innate disposition to accept risk and uncertainty in the fog of war and yet strike out boldly.

If the Indian Army needs one thing today, it is this risk-taking orientation in a rigid and overcautious army. Foreign military critics have castigated us for this lack of boldness and overcaution in our recent wars. Bangladesh was a golden exception. We dared, we took bold risks and we won a tremendous victory.

The Dharma Yudha or Just War Concept

The second aspect is highlighted by the very conscious concern of the Pandavas to be seen as the upholders of 'Dharma' or justice in this conflict. Their war, they were very keen to emphasize, was a just war. It was fought on certain ethical principles. Can modern statecraft be based on such ethical guidelines? The *Mahabharata* teaches a valuable lesson. The state propagandists must spare no effort to convince their own people and their armed forces that they are engaged in the defence of a 'just cause'. This acts as a tremendous fillip for civil and military morale. In fact the insistence on establishing the righteousness of their cause indicates the clear grasp of the *Mahabharata* leadership of the aspects of national and military morale.

Soldiers fight better if they are convinced of the cause they are fighting for. The political and military leadership should be acutely conscious of this factor. They must take great pains to propagate their cause and convince their citizenry and population that it is a just and righteous cause. This draws out the best in men. Motivation stems from conviction. Morale today has been upgarded to the level of a principle of war. No amount of equipment can compensate for any deficiency of morale. Morale is built-up and sustained by a conscious effort. The modern nation state resorts to a total effort to mobilize support by intensive propaganda beamed at both domestic and foreign audiences.

When viewed in this light the painstaking efforts made by the Pandavas to establish the justice or righteousness *(Dharma)* of their cause make a lot of sense. Even in today's context, men cannot be treated as push-button machines. They have to be motivated and the righteousness of their cause must be vigorously expounded to them by the state media. The Second World War saw the art of propaganda pushed to its ultimate levels.

In 1971 not only the Indian people and the Indian Armed Forces, but the whole world was convinced of the justice and righteousness of the Indian cause. India stayed her hand. She waited for almost eight months in the face of a mounting refugee influx. She moved in only when she was attacked in the West. Here we have the modern variant of the *Mahabharata* concept of a just or righteous war.

The onus of providing a clear *casus belli* is left to the adversary. In many ways, this was similar to the Soviet concept of the 'Virtuous Defence'. Soviet military theory specified that the fact of aggression must clearly be identified before it is responded to. Once the enemy has attacked, or hard intelligence indicates the strong probability of such an attack, the Soviet state was justified in unleashing its all-out counterattack (the theatre strategic offensive) to transfer the war to the enemy's territory as rapidly as possible.

The Indian state would do well to evolve such an offensive-defence philosophy and adopt 'Dharma' (or justice and righteousness) as the basis of its politico-military philosophy. Even the Americans in the post-Cold War phase have seriously deliberated upon the need for establishing an ethical basis for their foreign policy. The support for the Samozas and Marcoses and such oppressive, tinpot dictators has therefore been replaced by an emphasis on democracy. Corazino Aquinos and Benazirs have come in its aftermath.

What is of essence is the need to convince domestic and international audiences of the correctness or righteousness of the national cause. This calls for a concerted mobilization of national information resources and mass media to propagate this cause. Nations cannot prosecute wars in the absence of such a conscious mobilization. Hence the need to study the *Mahabharata* concept of 'just war'. At the very least, it highlights the cynical importance of painting the enemy as 'black' and ourselves as 'lily white'. This helps national morale, and morale is a war-winning factor. It was so in the time of the *Mahabharata* — it remains so today. This is an eternal principle and the entire epic deals with such eternal issues.

The author would like to conclude by asking for a major research effort to establish the historicity of the events and places mentioned in the Indian epics. We need to study our past to understand our present and evolve the shape of things to come in our future. The tremendous recent popularity of the electronic rendition of these epics only highlights the deep influence that they exercise on the collective Indian psyche. Modern-day nation builders and cultural revivalists have no option but to study this monumental epic. Indian soldiers need to study this work to understand the basis of their military heritage, and to gain insights that will enable them to develop an Indian school of war.

13

The Zeitgeist of the Mahabharata

The Age of Endism

Zeitgeist is a German word that means the moral and ethical tone of an age. The zeitgeist of the Mahabharata period is surprisingly similar to the zeitgeist, to the degenerate moral and ethical tone of our present Industrial Civilization. At the philosophical level there is a deep tonal similarity that is surprising. The Indian philosophical tradition offers a very cogent explanation. The era of the Mahabharata was classified as the era of the "Yuganta". Yuganta stands for the end of an era or an Age. The period of the Mahabharata was the period of the end of a millennium. An age was slowly winding down. An old order was nearing its end. Degeneration had set in, a moral and cultural decay had started. Righteousness was on the decline. The old order was crumbling — the new one that would replace it had not yet appeared. The Indian philosophical tradition speaks of four great cycles or Ages of civilization. These occur successively as :-

- Satya Yuga - The Age of Truth
- Dwapar Yuga - The Second Age
- Treta Yuga - The Third Age
- Kali Yuga or the Age of Iron and Machines. This is the present Industrial civilization that is also nearing its end.

The Mahabharata War occurred in the transition era between the Treta Age and heralded the onset of the present Kali Yuga or Industrial civilization. The ethical tone of the Mahabharata compares poorly with the lofty moral and ethical standards enshrined in the earlier Indian epic of the *Ramayana*. That was the age based on Truth. The moral and ethical decline of the Mahabharata period is self-evident. It stemmed from a glorification of the Self. Rural and pastoral society was giving way to large towns and city-states, which were the foci of capital accumulation and wealth formation. Over-vaulting ambition, greed, envy, jealousy, coveteousness, lust, and a fierce competitiveness, all these were all leit motifs of the Mahabharata civilization. The greed and avarice, the lust for the riches and women of other folks, the envy and pride and arrogance are writ large in the fabric of the tale. Selfishness is at its peak. Self-centeredness leads to fierce struggle and competition — to deep-seated rivalries, animosities and hatreds. This rise of negative emotions (as opposed to the positive and loftier emotions of altruism, self-sacrifice, generosity, compassion, and non-violence in thought, word and deed, and non-coveteousness etc.) is a characteristic of the end of an age or an era. It is the primal tonal hue of the *Mahabharata* epic. Indian civilization had reached an apogee of its cultural development and was then on the decline.

Armageddon

It had remained static for too long. Great churning movements were taking place in the depths of its collective psyche. The massive rise of greed, lust, avarice and other negative emotions was steadily leading the civilization to a great and terrible churning — to an Armageddon that would bring to the fore the deep seated moral and ethical contradictions of the age and lead it to destroy itself in one cataclysmic upheaval. There is in the Mahabharata that sense of helplessness before that collective civilisational doom. There is that feeling of fatalism. Like a Greek tragedy, it is all pre-ordained and pre destined. The slide towards a terrible fratricidal war, a horrific Armageddon is inevitable and inexorable. It cannot be avoided. This nemesis was bound to overtake the entire Indian civilization - come what may.

The Birth of the Prophetic Life Form

Krishna — the Grand Stategist of this Mahabharata War was aware of the future. He was a Prophetic being, a "Kala Purusha", an evolutionary higher form of life that was Prophetic — that could sense the coming future events. Krishna was a great visionary — he mapped out the path of the civilization. He sensed its rottenness and inner decay. The old order must be swept aside before the new is born. He operated at many levels. At one, he was the arch diplomat, feverishly engaged in trying to stave off this terrible, fratricidal war. He undertook desperate diplomatic missions to bring about a last minute compromise solution. The Pandavas would settle for just five villages - he told Duryodhana but to no avail.

The Paradoxical Approach

Paradoxically, at a far deeper level, Krishna was aware of the futility of this peace mission. War was indeed inevitable. He had seen it coming clearly. He was a Prophetic life form, an evolutionary mutant who could intuitively sense the coming events. And such events have a terrible finality about them. That age, that civilization had to be destroyed. It was on its way to decline and ultimate doom in a terrible cataclysmic conflict. In a strange paradoxical fashion, the Prophet of Peace was at once the terrible horseman of the Apocalypse. He deliberately shaped and engineered the events that would lead to that terrible fratricidal war. In a methodical way he ranged the best "Jedi Knights" of that era (the best car warriors and archers) against one another — in a manner that was designed to ensure their mutual destruction. Carefully he ranged the antagonistic forces for the Apocalyptic battle. Methodically he weaved the agenda of individual hatreds, envies and vendettas into the skein of an awful and cataclysmic conflict. The awful nature of these psychic events that were coming - he revealed to his disciple Arjuna. Such psychic tides are far too powerful for any puny human to change their course or withstand them. Arjuna, as the archetypal man, must play out his destined role. He must fulfill his destiny. The Queen mother of the Kurus, Gandhari, accused Krishna of deliberately engineering the Kurukshetra War so that the greatest military rivals to the supremacy of his Yadava democratic clans would destroy themselves mutually and leave the field clear for his Republican Yadava State. Mahabharata was the quintessential war where Krishna deliberately arrayed the most powerful monarchial powers of India against one another - so that they would be destroyed. Once these monarchial powers were eliminated - Krishna's Yadava clans would automatically gain pre-eminence in the Indian sub-continent.

As a paradoxical piece of a strategy it was astounding; It was grand strategy par excellence. Almost three millenniums later Britain would try to pit Nazi Germany against Stalins Soviet Union - so that these two over militarized, autocratic states would destroy one another in the Armageddon of the Second World War. The Democracies, in specific UK and USA thereby emerged triumphant and pre-ponderant at the end of this war. Nazi Germany was destroyed. The Soviet Union was mortally wounded. Four decades later it simply suffered an economic collapse due to imperial over, reach and over-stretch.

Conflict Avoidance Strategy

This Conflict Avoidance Strategy is far, far superior in essence to direct military strategy. Hadn't the Chinese sage Sun Tzu said, "For to fight and win all your battles is not the acme of excellence. Supreme excellence lies in subduing the enemy without fighting". Krishna's strategy to ensure the primacy of the democratic Yadava Republics in the Mahabharata period hinged upon subtly encouraging the two great monarchial alliances of the Kauravas and the Pandavas to decimate one another in a mutually destructive war. All the while, Krishna and his clans remained neutral (He participated as an advisor and charioteer only — not as a combatant). He ensured that the greatest car warriors of that age, the greatest archers, the greatest Jedi Knights were pitted against one another so that the mutual destruction would be thorough and complete. That left the field clear for the primacy of his Yadava Clans. The Queen Gandhari saw through this conflict avoidance strategy of Krishna, and his subtle engineering of the Kurukshetra War. What she misunderstood was the motive. Krishna did not act from the standpoint of personal interest or limited personal gains. He acted from the far superior standpoint of the sage who had foreseen the coming events. This age was winding down. This civilization was winding down. It had to be brought to a swift and decisive end so that the stage was set for the onset of a new millennium and a new age. He thought not in terms of individual life spans but in civilizational cycles.

The sophistication of this strategy is highlighted by the fact that Democracies of Great Britain and the USA consciously practiced it during the Second World War. The USA, tried to stay out of this conflict as long as possible. Its massive military industrial complex sought to maximize its profits by sale of arms to Europe. The prime strategy was to make the two mighty military war machines of that era (Nazi Germany and Stalin's Russia) get locked up in a mutually destructive Armageddon that would ensure their annihilation. This would (and this did) serve to leave the field clear for the subsequent emergence of the USA as the sole super power. The sophistication and superiority of this Conflict Avoidance Strategy is borne out by the statistical analysis of the casualities suffered by the various participants of the Second World War.

Soviet Union	-	25 million killed
Germany	-	07 million killed
Japan	-	02 million killed
USA	-	0.48 million killed
UK	-	0.34 million killed

The cummulative casualities of the USA and UK were less than one million dead. Contrast this with the horrific figures of 25 million Russians and 7 million Germans killed. Militarily the Allies were inefficient. They relied on attrition as opposed to a maneuvre-based strategy. It was their politico-military grand strategy however that was brilliant. Its central core was conflict avoidance and pushing other rival power centers into mutually destructive collisions that left them totally exhausted, drained and enfeebled. Paradoxically, Britain was too small a nation to withstand even the margins of this conflict. This British Empire was exhausted and crumbled at the end of World War II. The USA emerged as the primal global power simply because its competitors were severely debilitated by the mutual blood letting of the Second World War.

Even Krishna's Yadavas Clans (which emerged as the primal powers after the exhaustion of the Mahabharata War) did not long survive the aftermath of the Armageddon. Classical symptoms of civilizational decline appeared. The absence of any political or military challenge led to a massive drain of their creative energies in collective orgies (of the type that presaged the end of the Roman Empire).

The Glorification of the Self

The prime leit motif of the Mahabharata Society was the glorification of the self. The Vedic pastoral and forest civilization had given way to an urban civilization of city-states along the great River valleys of the Ganga, the Yamuna, the Sindhu and the Saraswati. The quest for opulent and grand palaces, for luxurious lifestyles, for gold and jewels and the lust for beautiful and voluptuous women were the liet motifs of that age. These city-states were the foci of capital formation and the accumulation of wealth. Their hedonistic life styles seemed to mirror the Zeitgeist of the Industrial Age of today. Today, Liberal Capitalism is the ruling ideology. Its central credo is "Greed is Good" and "More is not enough". It leads to fierce competition for the limited resources and goods, for access to and control of markets. When this quest, this unbridled competition for colonies and captive market gets out of hand - it can lead to Armageddons like the First and the Second World War. These wars were caused by the competitions going totally out of control. The Zeitgeist of the Industrial Civilization today with its credo of selfishness and hedonism, its glorification of Capitalism and market forces and its unbridled competition, is exactly the Zeitgeist of the Mahabharata era. The similarity of the moral and ethical tone is so surprising in essence.

The reason is that both the Mahabharata Age and the Industrial Civilization are terminal orders - civilizations in moral, ethical and social decay. The Industrial civilization today is based upon the fast depleting energy base of fossil fuels. These can last at best for another century. As they deplete, it will lead to fierce competition for the control of these fossil fuel reserves. In the meantime populations will boom. By the middle of the next century these will be more than doubled. The earth's resources will be strained to the limit. The fragile Eco-systems of the earth may get totally disturbed and disrupted. Pure Malthusian logic tells us that the Industrial Civilization is doomed. It is inexorably heading for an Armageddon, a terminal Apocalypse-even as the Mahabharata War was one. Will the Industrial Armageddon lead to a destruction of the Urban Civilization and a return to a more Green and Eco-friendly age — where fossil fuels are replaced by Green and renewable sources of energy — by solar sails and Hydrogen Fuel Cells? Technology, as we know it, may give way to Biotechnology. The linear Paradigm of the Industrial era will have to give way to the Fractal forms of nature. Man must learn to plug in to its supportive life cycles and food chains. He must not destroy the fragile Eco-system of the earth. Will an Armageddon be necessary to wipe the planetary stage clear of its dinosaurian Industrial infrastructure and mega cities? Massive changes in society do not occur in the absence of conflict - said Alwyn Toffler. Today there are a plethora of cultural prophecies about an approaching Armageddon. These may well turn out to be self-fulfilling. We are living in a "Yuganta" era. We are living in the end of a millennium. Expectations of an epochal conflict may, in the end, actually bring about such a conflict. It all depends on the stand point of the individual observer.

The Mahabharata is such an epic of endism. It was written at the end of another millennium. Hence the overarching relevance of its message for our day and age.

14

Visions of Apocalypse : The Philosophy of Endism

Yuganta : The Mindset of "Endism"

The age of the Mahabharata War was the age of "Yuganta"; it was the end of an age or an era. Even as these words are being written, we have just passed the end of the millennium. In purely ideological terms, the Mahabharata represents the first ideological clash between the political systems of democratic and republican clan rule (as followed by the Yadavas and in some ancient "Ganarajayas" in pre-historic India) and the absolute monarchial system based on hereditary rule. In this ancient war, we see the primal democrat Krishna following a masterly strategy of winning without engaging in combat. Centuries ago, the Chinese sage Sun Tzu had said, "For to fight and win all your battles is not the acme of excellence. Supreme excellence lies in subduing your enemy without fighting". Krishna's grand strategic approach was to engineer a titanic clash between the two antagonistic monarchial powers of his age and their alliance systems. As stated in the last chapter, the Allies at the commencement of World War II followed the same sophisticated strategy. They did their best to divert Nazi Germanys military fury towards Stalin's Soviet Union. The two rival totalitarian states nearly destroyed one another-thus leaving the field free for the democracies led by the USA to emerge. The final triumph for democracy and the liberal capitalist free market ideology came in the 1990s with the economic collapse of the Soviet Union. Francis Fukuyama proclaimed this ideological victory as the "End of History". His concept of endism created a stir in academic circles. Fukuyama clarified that the victory of Capitalism did not mean a literal full stop to the progression of events. It meant the logical culmination of a cycle of development which had come to an end with the triumph of the democratic-free market form of government over totalitarian state systems like Left Wing Communism and Extreme Right Wing forms like Nazism and Fascism. To that extent the present millennium is also an era of endism. History is cyclic. Its patterns tend to repeat and perpetuate themselves in cycles. It is amazing to learn that the Mahabharata War was also fuelled by such an ideological conflict between Clan democracies and Republican rule versus the absolute, hereditary monarchial political system of Ancient India. As a result of the Mahabharata war, clan republics became the dominant political form in North Western India. This continued through the Later Vedic Period and the early stages of Buddhism. Many of these Republican clan democracies suffered heavily during the invasion of Alexander (327-324 BC). This resulted in a political vaccum into which Chandragupta Maurya stepped in easily to consolidate the political unification of India under strong centralised and absolute monarchial rule.

Patterns of the Past : Predictions of the Future

Single event predictions are very difficult to make. In Forecasting techniques, it is far more reliable to go in for pattern predictions than for single event predictions. In the last chapter, we established that the Zeitgeist (the ethical and moral tone) of the Mahabharata age was very similar to the "Zietgiest" of our present Industrial civilisation. Both were premised upon a hedonistic glorification of the self - on self-assertion, greed and acquisitiveness. This generated competition and the negative emotions of jealousy, envy, hatred, and avarice. These were causative factors for war and Armageddon.

Depending upon what age we ascribe to the Mahabharata War - almost three or more millenniums later we are forced to ask ourselves this basic question. Are we headed for another Armageddon today? Are we sliding towards another terrible Apocalypse? A pattern analysis indicates that we are living today in an era of Endism - in an age of "Yuganta". The Industrial civilisation is winding down. It is reaching a terminal point of crisis and no return. How? Why?

The Collision of Curves

The facts are amazingly simple : The Industrial civilisation is powered by fossil fuels. These are a very limited and fast depleting resource. Current forecasts indicate that the world's reserves of oil will last at best for another 40-50 years, the reserves of Natural Gas for 75 years and of coal for just a 100-150 years more. The same critical position is true of some critical metallic ores. Even as the fossil fuels are depleting — the world is rapidly industrialising. More and more third world countries are entering the industrial age. The demand for fossil fuels is escalating rapidly. When a civilisation is premised on the fix of very high energy density fossil fuels, that are a finite and rapidly diminishing resource, the competition for the use and control of such resources can easily spin out of control.

The rapid boom in the earth's population further reinforces the trend towards conflict. As per United Nations forecasts - this is likely to double to over 11 billions by the middle of the next century.

These two curves — the rising curve of population and the steeply diving curve of fossil fuel availability are likely to collide well before the mid point of the 21st century. These antagonistic curves of resource depletion and population boom — can only lead to one Malthusian conclusion — war and conflict are inevitable on an unprecedented global scale.

Ecological Disaster

That is not all. As we are rapidly burning out the scarce fossil fuel reserves, we are unfixing the carbon from the earth's surface and subsurface and releasing it back into the terrestrial atmosphere. This means that in 50 years all the world's oil, in 75 years all the world's natural gas and in a 100 years all the worlds' coal would have been BURNT back into the earth's atmosphere. Evolution took millions of years to fix the carbon from the earth's atmosphere into the surface and subsurface by the process of photosynthesis. In just two centuries man will have burnt it all back. What will this lead to? Ecological catastrophes on an unprecedented scale. Global warming and the Green house effect. The melting of the polar ice caps and the rise of the level of the ocean; the flooding of the low-lying coastal areas and island territories. This could lead to the severe disruption of the earth's fragile ecosystems. A century more of this carbon burning, and this planet's atmosphere would resemble that of Venus or Mars. Both are dead and inert planets. Isn't this self-evident? Don't we all know these grim facts? It is amazing that despite this knowledge there is no alarm. There is only a mad, lemming like race amongst third world countries to industrialise, to urbanise and to transform their civilisations in the image of the West. There is a mass uprooting of humanity from the countryside to the cities and slums of the metropolitan centers. There are the psychological mal effects of overcrowding and the compression of individual spaces for self-expression. No one has colonised Mars as yet. Nor is anyone likely to do so in the foreseeable future. The world does not have the migration safety net that cushioned the first doubling of the world population. The writing therefore is on the wall. We are heading for an Armageddon. We are heading for an Apocalypse. We are heading inexorably for the terminal crisis of the Industrial Civilisation.

The problem is that the old order is so deeply entrenched that it refuses to go away. There are billions of dollars locked up in the industrial infrastructure; in the electrical power grids, in the oil refineries and tankers; in the storage tanks and pipelines, in the refining, cracking and extraction industries. This old and entrenched order will refuse to go away - even if it means the end of this earth. It will perhaps have to be destroyed or deconstructed before we can erect the edifice of a new civilisation that is clean and GREEN, that is based upon the energy base of Renewable and Green sources of energy - on hydrogen in its pure form or solar energy in its many variants.

We may have to transform and reinvent our civilisation into a more ecological, more dispersed and less urbanised form if we wish to survive as a species. We may have to replace crowded cities with Swiss style Cantons. Replace the factories with the home as a work place; replace the consumer and producer with a "prosumer" and switch from industrial and electronic technology to Biotechnology and Bionics.

The birth of bionics will not occur without pain and conflict. Massive changes in society, said Toffler — do not occur in the absence of war and conflict. It is precisely this conflict that the Mahabharata epitomises — the conflict of Yuganta — the conflict that ends an age. The industrial civilisation is now on a terminal curve of self-destruction. It can not coexist with the fractal order of nature. The linear paradigm of the straight lines epitomises the industrial civilisation. Witness its straight sky scapers, its straight highways and rail-roads, its grid pattern cities, its endless blocks of urban settlements. Man masterted the Geometry of the straight line and in his exuberance tried to enforce it on all nature. Much later, he learnt that nature is not based on chaos. It is based on a much higher order of mathematics that is Non-linear and Fractal in form, that can repeat itself endlessly, that is not based on struggle, conflict and competition, but a systems approach based on symbiosis, harmony and cooperation.

That then is the quintessential message of the myth of the Mahabharata. Situations and patterns repeat themselves endlessly. They are fractal in form. That is why their mathematical form tends to repeat itself in a cyclic fashion. We are living in the era of Endism — not just the end of a millennium but the end of an age — the end of a civilisation — the end of the Industrial order. Such ends are cataclysmic; they do often culminate in a civilisational Armageddon or Apocalypse. That is the theme of the Mahabharata.

Myths and the Minds of Men

Wars and Armageddon, says the Mahabharata, occur first in the minds of men. It is there that we have to look for the causative factors and symptons that presage the onset of the systemic crisis. The Mahabharatan civilisation was premsied on the hedonistic assertion of the Self. It glorified the self. Possibly, it epitomised the modern Industrial and Capitalistic concepts of "Greed is good" and "More is not enough". Such self-assertive tendencies lead to competition and conflict. We need to emulate the Green systems approach of nature that is more altruistic, that is based on symbiotic bonds and supportive relationships. We should not thoughtlessly destroy what we do not fully understand. We should not disrupt the food chains and Eco-systems of the biosphere. We should not wreak havoc with its fine tuned systems of checks and balances. We should not disrupt the feedback loops. The Western metaphors of rape the earth and subdue Nature are a trifle outdated. In glorifying them we are collectively travelling down the road to catastrophe.

If we go on unchecked on this road-one-day our living planet, this Green Gaia, may well resemble the arid Martian landscape. That is the grim philosophical message of the Mahabharata. That is the keynote of this civilisational myth. Let us not forget the deep psychological truth. For the myth is the basis of reality.

Expectations of an Epochal Conflict

The Mahabharata was an epochal war that marked the end of a phase of civilisational development. It was a self-destructive Malthusian exercise. We have just passed the end of a Millennium. The last century (with its two world wars) was the bloodiest in all human history. Today, the Industrial Civilisation seems to be winding down as fossil fuel reserves are over-used and deplete rapidly. A large number of culture specific prophecies (like those of Nastradamus) warn of a third Armageddon or Apocalypse. Will this come to pass? It depends upon the strength of the underlying and entrenched belief. How much percentage of the human population expects such an epochal conflict to occur. That will determine whether it comes to pass or not. The Mahabharata is such an exercise in Pattern predictions. It represents the philosophy of Endism — the end of an era, the end of a Millennium — the end of the Industrial civilisation or the "Kaliyuga". The past and future tenses blend strangely in this epic. It is the primal repositary of the Indian Military Art and Tradition.

Epilogue

Psychological Analysis

To delve into the psychological roots of the Indian military ethos, we must undertake a study of the monumental epic of the *Mahabharata*. It has rightly been called a 'national epic'. It is national in the sense that it seeks to define India as not just a civilizational but a definitive political entity called Bharata. Its final rendition was commissioned in the Golden Age of Indian history when the Guptas caused an official version of this epic to be written. It is this that accounts for the standardization of the texts found in various parts of the country. It celebrates the theme of an imperial Indian past of grandeur. It celebrates the fact that India is one – from Gandhara in the West to Magadha and Angadesha in the East; from Panchnad in the North to Dakshina Patha in the South. The *Mahabharata* is the story of an Indian Armageddon.

Many authors have drawn parallels between Indian and Greek mythology. Thus, Sister Nivedita in her book *The Footfalls of Indian History* has quoted Megasthenes (the Greek Ambassador to Chandragupta's court) to highlight the similarities between the Greek legend of Heracles and the Indian legend of a superhuman Krishna. Both are credited with having lifted and kept aloft a mountain, and a world respectively. The Indian core legend of *Ramayana* has the beautiful Sita being abducted across the seas. The basic thematic similarity with the *Iliad* is interesting. Does it point to a set of core racial myths of the Aryan people that predate their Diaspora? The myth of the 'Great Flood' is also common to many religions and cultures.

Going by the tenets of Jung's psychology, these core myths have a universal or archetypal character. They are the collective inheritance of races. They are lodestars buried deep in the collective unconscious of a people. They have a strange and inexorable influence. The myth in some incomprehensible way becomes the basis of reality. There seems to be a compulsive collective urge to act out this myth, time and again in real life to live it out, again and again. The compulsions of the race are deep-rooted and psychological.

That is why a purely historical treatment of the myth of the *Mahabharata* by itself does not suffice. A deeply ingrained myth of an Armageddon may impel a people to play out that war in the psyche, in the form of a grand military conflict. Such deep-rooted and compulsive psychological attitudes may well cause yet another war on the subcontinent before the end of this decade of the new millennium. That is why it is essential to be aware of the psychological backdrop of current attitudes and belief systems. It is essential to analyse the contents of our own 'Weltanschauung' before they begin to impel us inexorably into the playing out of our racial myths of a mighty war.

That is why in the concluding chapter, it is essential to delve into the psychological basis of the myth of the *Mahabharata*. The myth is dominated by characters of archetypal dimensions.

Vyasa, the chronicler, flits in and out of his own creation – like some strange will-o'-the-wisp. He not only chronicles history but also plays a major part in creating it. His physical intervention, at crucial periods of the narrative, is decisive. Vyasa, in Jungian psychology, may well represent the archetypal figure of the 'wise old man'. Here, again, we find another facet of the uniquely Indian legend of Vishnu – the revivalist aspect of Hindu consciousness. A Sanskrit verse says 'Vyasa verily is Vishnu – Vishnu is Vyasa.' Vyasa, incidentally, is not a name. It is a historical title conferred upon a great scholar whose works help in preserving and perpetuating the Indian tradition. Thus, the real name of the author of *Mahabharata* is Rishi Krishna Dwaipayan. He is an intellectual giant and a great compiler of the hitherto oral tradition. He is called Ved Vyasa because he finally reduced the four Vedas to the written form. The *Mahabharata*, his original and creative rendition of his life and times, is his 'fifth Veda'. It is born of his deep reflection and introspection on the epoch-making events of the age that he lived in. This great intellectual feat that serves to preserve the Indian cultural inheritance confers upon him the title of Vyasa – the form of Vishnu – the great preserver of the Indian pantheon. We need to study this aspect of the Vishnu legend in more detail, for it explains the basis of the marvellous assimilative and regenerative potential of Indian civilization. The Indian civilization survives because it is constantly renewed, and recharged in thought, ideological content, and in action.

Who is the real hero of the *Mahabharata*? Is it Lord Krishna extolled as the eighth incarnation of Vishnu or is it Arjuna – the great warrior and the world's greatest archer? Another school feels that Karna, the eldest of the Pandava children, is the real hero of this great epic. All three personages are Indian personality archetypes and merit a detailed look. Shakespeare's plays indicate a tremendous psychological insight. Thus, *Hamlet* is an excellent dramatization of the Oedipal conflict in man, the suppressed libidinal attachment to the mother which is transformed into hate as a reactive psychological defence mechanism. *Julius Caesar* gives us a tremendous insight into mob psychology, and *Macbeth* deals with guilt and overvaulting ambition.

The *Mahabharata* is full of such psychological insights. The characterization is vivid and multidimensional. The principle actors are etched in all their psychological complexity. The India psychological make-up is more complex. The Western theme of Oedipal conflict (that becomes the battleground of the emerging adolescent personality) is only partially applicable in the Indian context. It is compounded by the fact that the Indian father dotes upon his son much more than his Western counterpart. This only serves to accentuate the primordial conflict. The Indian son, in suppressing his Oedipal/incestuous urges, transforms them into worship of the father. Thus Parashurama, the terrible sage and sixth incarnation of Vishnu, beheads his mother on the orders of his father. The Indian mother in turn loves her male progeny with an intensity that borders on distraction. This can only be understood if we realize that, in the Indian cultural context, the birth of a male offspring represents her fulfilment. With this as the psychological backdrop, let us analyse the principal characters of this epic.

Krishna is the Indian Heracles. He is one of the most charismatic Indian personages ever to stalk the cultural landscape. To the Indians, he is God in human form. Not only is he a great warrior, he is also a great sage. He is 'Partha-Sarathi', the charioteer and friend of Arjuna, who propagated the philosophy of the *Upanishads* for the Indian masses. His *Bhagavad Gita* is an exquisite treatise that synthesizes all the existing Indian schools of philosophy, and propagates them in a universal form – a perennial message for all men of action. The ideology of supreme skill in action as an end in itself, is the finest motivational basis for fighting ever devised. The *Gita* has been preached in the middle of a battlefield – not in some remote and cloistered monastery. Krishna is a great statesman, a great strategist, the founder of democracy in India in an age when hereditary, kings ruled the roost, a great general, Pluto's version of a philosopher-king and, last but not the least, a great lover. He is the Indian ideal of manhood. He is the Indian Animus figure of perfection – the divine lover not just to Radha of his generation, but to Meera centuries later. His amorous themes are woven into the Indian classical ballads and dance forms even today. In times of great crises, the Indian civilization passionately and ardently seeks such a great and charismatic leader that they cannot only follow but worship also.

Arjuna is the favourite of his mother, his brothers and his *guru* (teacher). He is handsome, brave and accomplished. He is 'born to win'. It is his ambition to become the world's greatest archer. In the end he becomes the greatest warrior of the subcontinent and defeats the greatest heroes of his age. He is regarded by many as the prima donna of the *Mahabharata*. He proves the psychological dictum that the son, who is the favourite of his mother, acquires that crucial psychological edge. He is primed to 'win' in life. At the philosophical level, Arjuna represents the 'Jivaatma' (the individual soul) and Krishna the Paramatman (the cosmic consciousness). Arjuna is another version of the Indian Animus.

Karna is possibly the most complex and beautifully etched character of this epic. In a strange way, he ends up as its hero. He is Kunti's first born. However, he is an illegitimate child, and his mother rejects him at birth. This rejection and loss of a mother's love, is a psychological trauma that haunts him throughout his life. The American psychologist, Erich Fromm has beautifully highlighted the trauma of the loss of 'mother's love'. It colours the basic script of the individual's life. He becomes a 'born loser'. However great be his achievements and accomplishments, he is primed to self destruction. He must fulfil his basic script of being a born loser. He lost his first 'battle' for the love of his mother. He extrapolates from this primal defeat and extends it to every sphere of his life. He will reach the very pinnacle of success only to stop short and destroy himself – just to justify his psychological 'script'. Karna truly is the world's greatest archer. Even Krishna acknowledges his greatness. He is brave and noble and generous to a fault. He is tormented by his alleged 'low birth'. He is denied his rightful place in the sun. Duryodhana sees his potential, befriends him and makes him a king. For this, his gratitude is intense and life long. Karna is the tormented hero forever seeking the great battle, the final war where he will redeem himself. Treachery goes against his noble grain and the perfidy of Shakuni disgusts him. He is the archetypal warrior, the son of the Sun God, quick to temper and irascible. His generosity is legendary, and as bountiful as the light of the sun that falls freely on everyone. The final torture comes when just before the war his mother (on Krishna's instigation) reveals to him the secret of his birth. He cannot now kill his brothers, and promises this to his mother – he will spare all except the hated rival Arjuna. In the end Karna is not killed justly in straight combat. The great warrior is slain when he is without his arms – in gross violation of the tradition of chivalry. The son, who lost his mother's love, has destroyed himself in keeping with his personalized myth.

Bhima, more truly the Indian Heracles, is the middle born. He epitomizes the trauma of this psychological archetype. The first born is the favourite of the father, the youngest of the mother – the middling boy feels unloved and discarded. The *Mahabharata* abounds in such deep psychological insights that often provide a clue as to why a particular character acted in a particular way.

Draupadi and Kunti are the two grand dames who are very largely responsible for this war. They are imposing and regal personalities and testify to the high position of women in the Indian society of that time. Draupadi is a ravishing beauty desired by all – a *femme fatale* who may be regarded as the archetypal Indian 'Anima'. She arouses monumental passions. All kings desire her. So does Karna. She ridicules him, and chooses Arjuna. Karna never forgives her. She possibly objectifies his Oedipal conflict. He calls her a whore and encourages Duryodhana to humiliate her publicly. Draupadi's unkind laughter sears itself in the memory of Duryodhana. Her alleged barb about his father's blindness costs her very dearly. She is loved and hated with an intensity that borders on the bizarre. She is, in sum, one of the main causes of the war. A woman of strong character and indomitable will, she primes the Pandavas to seek revenge. She is a principal character in this epic.

Both Draupadi and Sita fit the Jungian concept of the Indian Anima —

or feminine archetype. Both these Indian heroines were the emblems of the concept of beauty and feminine qualities in their age. Most of the male cast of these epics projected their Animas on to these archetypal women. The projection of the Anima led to the psychological upheavals that they caused in the lives of the principal characters of these epics. Facing up to the anima implies facing ones own psychological reality and the deep seated flaws in our psychological makeup. The anima often externalises the deep seated conflicts latent in the human psyche. One of the most sophisticated tools of psychological warfare therefore is to confront a man with his anima. This was done in the epic of the Ramayana. Ravana, a great scholar and warrior was confronted with Sita. He projected his anima on to her and that led to the unraveling of his inner psychological makeup and strength. Sita proved to be his undoing and doom. Similarly, in the Mahabharata epic the Kaurava princes and Karna are confronted with their animas in the person of Draupadi. She proves to be the focus of their guilt and undoing. In the Shakespearian play "Julius Ceaser", we find the principal character Antony meeting his doom when he projects his anima on to Cleopatra — the queen of the Nile.

The hatreds that smoulder in the *Mahabharata* are the result of such thoughtless little acts that sear into the psychological depths of the principal actors. In the end, it is difficult to decide really as to who is more sinned against than sinning. The *Mahabharata* therefore is a valuable psychological document that helps us to understand and unravel the basic Indian character.

This psychological analysis has deliberately been appended in the end of this book. Though its historical value is little, it is essential to understand the myth per se. Psycho-history, or the psychological analysis of the great leaders of world history, is a recent but significant trend. Walter Langer's wartime psychoanalysis of Adolf Hitler (*The Mind of Adolf Hitler*) is a significant pointer.

The *Mahabharata* provides deep psychological insights into the Indian mind. A psychoanalysis of the principal characters of the *Mahabharata* highlights the strengths and weaknesses of their military character. It explains why they won or lost a particular battle. Sun Tzu said, 'Anger his general, confuse him and then strike.' Krishna's understanding of the character of the principal enemy commanders was impressive. He objectively analysed the flaws in their mental make-up. Thus Karna was irritable and short-tempered. Krishna used Salya to anger him. In a haze of confusion that great warrior performed at a tremendous disadvantage. The fatal flaw in Dronacharya's make-up was his extreme attachment to his son, Ashwathama. This was exploited to neutralize him by spreading the rumour that his son had been killed. In that state of shock the great teacher of war was killed by men who were no match for him in straight combat. Duryodhana was vain and impetuous. He would rush in like a fool where angels would fear to tread. His impetuosity caused him many humiliations on the battlefield.

The *Mahabharata's* ideal military commander, therefore, is calm and composed. This is the kind of cool courage that even Clausewitz has admired in his magnum opus. The hot-headed courage is short-lived. It may achieve much but it is not a sustained habit of character. Rash and purposeless displays of daring may temporarily enthuse an army, but in the long run they are counterproductive. The military character of Duryodhana has been used to highlight this fact time and again. A good general is like Giap – 'a snow-covered volcano'. He does not lose his head in a difficult situation. In a flux of shock and change, he is calm and imperturbable. To withstand the stresses and strains of combat, the *Mahabharata* laid great emphasis on a lofty character and calm temperament in a general. Each military commander develops his individual style of war in keeping with his basic temperament. His way of waging war has to be in tune with his character. He may be aggressive, bold and daring – or he may be rigid, over cautious and hesitant. This will leave an indelible imprint on his style of waging war. Thus, Patton, Sharon and Zhukov are examples of bold and aggressive generals. Rommel, Guderian and Manstein were cool, highly competent and great risk-takers. They were masters of mobile warfare. Montogomery personifies the rigid and overcautious British approach to generalship.

The *Mahabharata* provides us an Indian view of history based upon 'Avatarahood'. This needs to be elevated from its present primitive level of understanding to a more mature and scientific form. The so-called arrival of an *avatara* may just represent the onset of a social revolution that seeks to bring about a civilizational revival. Such a cultural renaissance comes about when a civilization is facing an external or internal crisis. A challenge from the social or cultural environment unleashes the synergy of a people. An *avatara*-like charismatic leader may act as the trigger for such a social revolution. Such a revolution, as the historian Iyengar puts it, may represent the 'march of God on earth'.

More than a military manual, the *Mahabharata* is an encyclopaedic record of the development of the Indian civilization. In this book, the author has focused entirely on the military aspects. That is why, in conclusion, it is essential to acknowledge the much wider scope and value of this monumental epic. It deserves more serious study by our scholars and academics. A text as vast as the *Mahabharata* needs to be treated with respect. It is indeed a 'National Epic' with a universal message. It is an invaluable psychological document. The battlefield of the Kurukshetra War, is allegorical of the battlefields in our individual minds where good battles with evil each day. The wars that we fight have their origin in the minds of men. They are externalizations of the basic psychological conflicts within. This in sum represents a holistic view of war per se.

However, beyond a scholastic study of war in its many dimensions, the study of the Mahabharata epic would be central to the development of Indology as a mature social discipline. The Mahabharata epic is encyclopedic in its sweep. It has a message and a relevance that goes far beyond the purely Indic. It has a message that is universal. The *Mahabharata* deals in essence, with an age of Endism. Its moral and ethical tone is so remarkably similar to the Zietgiest of our Industrial civilisation. Viewed as an interpretive essay in Pattern Prediction — the Mahabharata possibly points to the end of the industrial civilisation (or the age of Kali). It could easily be interpreted as a pattern prediction for an Armageddon in the Indian Sub-continent (a Fourth Indo-Pakistan War) and equally for a world wide Apocolypse in which a rising new Green ideology seeks to wipe out the entrenched industrial order.

Bibliography

"The Hymns of the Rig Veda" Translated by Ralph T.H. Griffith, II Vol., Second edition, Benaras 1896-97.

"The Veda of the Black Yajus School" (Taittertya Samanta) Translated by A.B. Keith, Two Volumes, Cambridge. Ross. 1914. (Harvard Oriental Series).

"Atharva Veda Samhita" Translated by W.D. Whitney, Revised and ed by C.R. Lanman, Cambridge, Mass 1905.

Mahabharata Ed. by Pancanana Tarkaratna (two vols), Calcutta, 1904.

Mahabharata Translated into English with Original Sanskrit Text by P.C. Roy, New Ed (Revised by S.L. Bahaduri), Calcutta 1919.

"Persian Translation of the Mahabharata" by Naquib Khan Faize and others (1720 AD). Original Manuscript with National Museum, New Delhi.

Kautilyas Arthashastra Revised and ed by R. Shamashastry, Mysore 1919.

Kautilyas Artha Shastra with Commentry Srimula by T Ganapathy Shastri, Trivandrum Sanskrit Series (Three Vols) Trivandrum 1924.

Sukracharya Nitisara Translated into English by B.K. Sarkar, Sacred Books of the Hindus, Allahabad 1914.

Agni Purana Ed by Pancanana Tarkaratna, Calcutta, 1907.

Garuda Purana Translated into English by Ernest Wood and S.V. Subramanyam, Sacred Books of the Hindus, Allahabad.

Dhanur Veda Samhita of Vaishista (with Hindi Translations) Ramraksha Pala, Bombay, 1902.

Ancient India as described by Megasthenes and Arrian J.W. McCrindle, London 1926.

The Invasion of India by Alexander the Great McCrindle, London 1896.

"Sun Tzu : The Art of War" Samuel B. Griffith.

Art of War in Ancient India P.C. Chakravarty (L.P.) Publications, Delhi 1941.

Kurukshetra War : A Military study, Maj. P. Sensarma, Naya Prakash, Calcutta, 1982.

Military Wisdom of the Puranas Maj P. Sensarama, Naya Prakash, Calcutta, 1984.

Numbers, Predictions and War Col. Trevor. N. Du Puy, Mac Donalds and Janes, London, 1979.

The Early History of India Vincent Smith, Oxford, 1941.

Footfalls of Indian History Margret Noble, Ramakrishna Mission Publications, Calcutta, 1932.

Encyclopaedia of the Red Army Maj. Gen. Shelford Bidwell, Pergemas and Brassey 1982.

The Collected Works of Carl. G. Jung Jung Carl Gustav, Prınceton University Press, Princeton.

Societies and Military Power : India and its Armies Stephen Peter Rosen. Cornell University, 1996.

Indian Strategic Thought : An Interpretive Essay. "George K. Tanham Rand Corporation Note No. R-4207-USDP, Prepared for the Under Secretary of Defence for Policy.

"*A Fire in the East*" Paul Bracken.

"A History of India". Herman Kulke and Deitmar Rothermund. Paperback edition. Routledge. London 1990.

"Ancient India : In Historical Outline" Dr. D.N. Jha. Manohar. New Delhi 2000.

"Horse and Elephant Armour" Dr. G.N. Pant, Agam Kala Prakashan. Delhi. 1997.

"Indian Arms and Armour", Dr. G.N. Pant, 3 Vols., Army Educational Stores, New Delhi.

Index

उद्यो० २६२

ततोहंतंनमस्कृत्यरथमारुह्यसत्वरः प्राध्मापयंरणेशंखंपुनर्हेमप
रिज्जिगीषया समेतस्मिन्‌रणे पूर्वे
नवभिःशराणांनतपर्वणां चत्वार
प्रतिरुद्धस्तथैवाहंसमरेदंशितस्थि
भ्योविशेषतः नमहंस्मयन्निवरणे
नितामेनिर्मर्यादेह्यपित्वपि भूय
ह्वे येतेवेदाःशरीरस्थाब्राह्मणएपंच
तेभ्यःप्रहराम्यहं प्रहरे क्षत्रधम
क्षत्रियत्वंहियातिशास्त्रमस्तुधमार
लंत्वंमे एषतेकार्मुकंवीरछिनद्मिनि
विक्षेपभरतर्षभ तेनास्यधनुषः
त्रिसप्तकानांशतानिनतपर्वणां वि